CORTEZ
CROSSROADS

A Guide to the
Anasazi Heritage
and Scenic Beauty
of the
Four Corners Region

Frederick W. Lange

Johnson Books: Boulder

Pub. 1989 - Call first for current info.

To the people of the Four Corners Area,
past, present, and future

Illustrations by Nick Lang

Cover illustration and design by Molly Davis

First Edition
1 2 3 4 5 6 7 8 9

ISBN 1-55566-052-5
LCCCN 89-63127

Printed in the United States of America by
Johnson Publishing Company
1880 South 57th Court
Boulder, Colorado 80301

PREFACE

The Four Corners area is the only place in the United States where four states (Colorado, New Mexico, Arizona, and Utah) come together in one spot. The surrounding areas also bring together a unique juxtaposition of mountains, deserts, prehistoric and historic sites to present a wealth of scenic, cultural, educational, and recreational opportunities.

My involvement with the Yellow Jacket Archaeological Project, the development of the Cortez CU Center, and related traveling exhibitions have provided me with frequent opportunities to travel widely and to lecture throughout the state of Colorado and the Rocky Mountain region. Wherever I went, I was asked where to go, what to see, and where to stay in this area. I came to realize that, while the different states and tourist organizations promoted their own limited spheres, there was nothing to help the visitor enjoy the bigger picture and the richness of opportunities in the Four Corners area.

The Four Corners truly unite, rather than divide, and the dramatic remains of the prehistoric Anasazi know no state boundaries. This guide is designed to encourage visitors to venture around the next corner, follow an unpaved road, and enjoy a sunset they might otherwise miss. While the emphasis is on the summer visitor, the beauty of the fall colors, and the exciting winter sports are also noted.

Cortez, the Center of the Anasazi World, is a logical hub for this region, a gateway to the many exciting areas surrounding it. I have selected the entries in the guide from a variety of sources and with the assistance of various travel organizations and chambers of commerce. No one has paid to be listed, and if a worthwhile business, park, or museum has been omitted, it has been, quite simply, an oversight.

I would like to thank the many people who contributed material and who checked the sections of this guide that pertained to their activities. Spe cial thanks to Tree Hayne, who typed the early versions of the manuscript, and to Nick Lang, who did the drawings. Any errors or omissions are my responsibility.

ABOUT THE AUTHOR

Frederick W. Lange is an archaeologist who has worked in the Four Corners region. He is dedicated to promoting the interpretation and protection of the rich cultural heritage of the area. Lange is Curator of Anthropology at the University of Colorado Museum in Boulder, an honorary citizen of Cortez, and a founding member of the board of directors of the Cortez Center, Inc. He has written a number of scholarly and popular publications, and is the co-editor of *Yellow Jacket: A Four Corners Anasazi Ceremonial Center* and *Among Ancient Ruins: The Legacy of Earl Morris*, also published by Johnson Books.

Contents

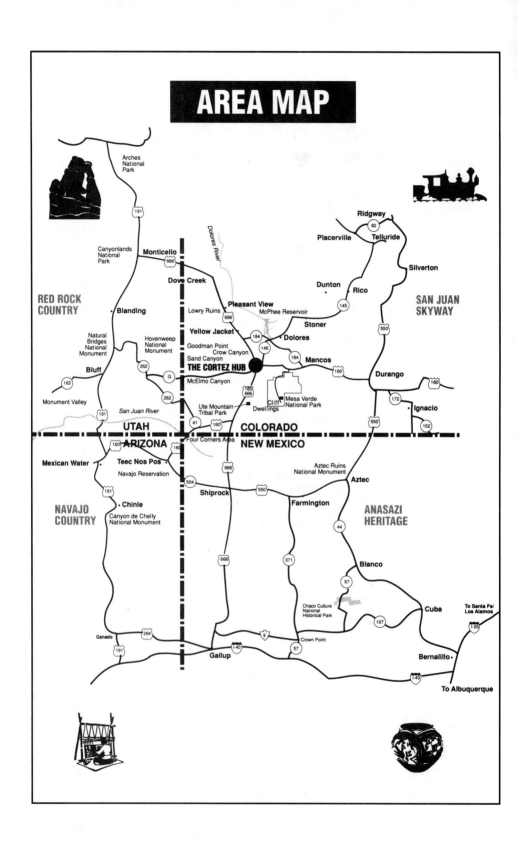

AREA MAP

PART 1
CORTEZ: HUB OF THE FOUR CORNERS AREA

▼▼▼▼▼▼▼▼▼▼

More visitors, American and foreign alike, come to southwestern Colorado every year to see the cliff dwellings of Mesa Verde National Park than for any other reason. They are beginning to learn, however, that in order to take advantage of an increasing number of opportunities to appreciate the cultural heritage and natural beauty of the Four Corners region, Cortez is the place to start.

The city of Cortez is the commercial and transportation hub of southwestern Colorado and the county seat of Montezuma County. It sits at an elevation of 6,200 feet. Originally settled by homesteaders in 1886, Cortez today has 9,000 residents. The city proudly lays claim to being the archaeological capital of the United States, and the multitude of foreign travelers among the more than 700,000 annual visitors reflects the worldwide popularity of the region.

Even the first prehistoric residents of the area must have appreciated the stunning scenery. Since the early eighteenth century the enduring mystery of the Anasazi ruins has attracted millions of travelers, explorers, and tourists. Strategically located near Mesa Verde National Park and other ruins, Cortez is also the commercial center for modern day Ute and Navajo Indians. Numerous local stores and galleries specialize in handmade Native American jewelry, rugs, and pottery. Local businesses and schools provide employment and educational opportunities.

Cortez is surrounded by some of the world's greatest scenery. Lush mountains meet sparse plateaus and even desert. To the east, the San Juan Mountains tower to over 12,000 feet. To the west, the High Sonoran Desert meets the evergreens and fertile soil of the Montezuma Valley. Mesa Verde is the most distinctive landmark of the area, surrounded by other majestic landforms such as Ute Mountain and the Chuskas, Lukachukais, and Abajo Mountains. All of these majestic features can be seen from Cortez and are less than a day's drive away. Wildlife in this area ranges from elk and deer to beaver and ground hogs.

In addition to the 900-year-old cliff dwellings at Mesa Verde National Park, there are thousands of other archaeological sites throughout the area. Between AD 900 and 1300 more than 40,000 people are thought to have lived within fifty miles of Cortez, then moved away, victims of climatic changes that made farming impossible. Prehistoric Anasazi life is studied and interpreted at the new Anasazi Heritage Center (just north of Cortez near Dolores), at the Cortez CU Center in Cortez, at the Mesa Verde Visitors Center, and at the Crow Canyon Archaeological Center, northwest of Cortez.

There is a wide range of natural resources in the Cortez area. Early in the twentieth century the rich soil of the Montezuma Valley supported agricultural expansion, and then came the cattlemen. Logging was a major industry until about 1930, and the 1940s saw the mining of uranium and other minerals. Coal, gas, and oil are the natural resources being exploited today. Agriculture continues to be an important contributor to the economy, particularly in alfalfa and pinto beans. The newly developed multicolored Anasazi Bean has its own intriguing taste and is being grown by local farmers. Souvenir bags and recipe books are available in local stores.

The other two major communities in Montezuma County, Dolores and Mancos, have about a thousand residents each. Total county population is about 20,000, considerably less than estimates of the Precolumbian population.

Just north of Cortez, the Dolores River was dammed to form the second largest body of water in Colorado. The McPhee Recreation Area lake has over 4,470 surface acres and was opened to boating and fishing in 1986. Above the reservoir, the Dolores River is a major recreation area where rainbow, brown, and cutthroat trout test the fisherman. Downstream from the dam, the rapids and the dramatic beauty of the Dolores River valley make rafting a memorable experience. Four smaller lakes within a thirty-minute drive of Cortez contain bass, pike, catfish, and the ever-present trout varieties.

At the Four Corners Monument, west of Cortez, you can stand in four states at one time: Colorado, New Mexico, Arizona, and Utah. This is the only place in the United States where four states come together. The monument is one hour from Cortez on Highway 160. The monument is within the Ute Mountain Ute and Navajo reservations, and a modest entrance fee is charged. Native American food and craft booths surround the monument.

Cortez is the hub of the Four Corners area, and from summer to fall, through winter and spring, the ever-changing face of the landscape offers different opportunities to appreciate the cultural heritage and natural beauty of the region. From the semiarid deserts to the plateaus and on to the high mountains above, there is something for everyone, all year-round.

Please do not contribute to the destruction of the rich prehistoric past of the Four Corners area by purchasing Native American artifacts from private individuals, shops, or galleries. There are excellent imitations and many reproductions (all of which should be marked or initialed by the contemporary artist) available for decorating bookshelves, offices, and mantels!

CORTEZ INFORMATION CENTERS

There are 800 motel rooms in Montezuma County and a dozen public and private campgrounds within easy driving distance of downtown Cortez. Restaurant menus cover the complete range of dining, from fast food to attractive full-service establishments.

The distinctive Colorado Welcome Center and Cortez Area Chamber of Commerce building is conveniently located on Main Street on the southeast corner of the City Park at the corner of Highway 160 and Mildred Road, across the street from the Cliff Dweller Gallery. The out-of-state toll-free number is 800-346-6528, or in-state (303) 565-3414.

The Colorado Welcome Center and Cortez Area Chamber of Commerce

This combined tourist and visitor facility provides information for those looking to get the most from their stay in this area and carries information about other Colorado destination as well. Maps, day trip guides, and information on lodging, restaurants, shopping, recreation, and travel are available in this authentic, southwestern-style building. Take time to relax and enjoy the exhibits from area artisans as well as pottery excavated from ancient ruins.

The University of Colorado has established a unique partnership with the Cortez community in order to promote education, especially in the field of archaeology. The CU Museum at the Cortez Center, located at 25 North Market Street, has exhibits from the Yellow Jacket site, the Ute Mountain Ute Park, and the Anasazi Heritage Center. Also featured are displays and photo murals of University of Colorado research in archaeology.

The Cortez CU Center and Museum

The museum is open daily, Monday through Saturday, during summer months, and on a more limited basis during the rest of the year. Watch for the brown and white MUSEUM signs on Main Street.

During the summer, the university and the center sponsor a biweekly evening series of illustrated talks on archaeology and other topics of cultural interest. Around the Fourth of July weekend every summer, the Center hosts an invitational painting show for local artists. A complete schedule is available by calling (303) 565-1151.

The Cortez CU Center is the point of origination for Anasazi Tours, a privately operated business. The Center maintains a growing library of video materials on southwestern prehistory, ethnology, and general science and is frequently utilized by local school teachers as an extension of classroom teaching. The Center Museum received an Exemplary Program Award from the National University Continuing Education Association (NUCEA) in 1989 and has also received private foundation and broad community support for its programs.

Anasazi Tours   A different and easy way to explore the ancient world of the Anasazi is offered by Anasazi Tours, based in Cortez. Anasazi Tours take visitors into the heartland of southwestern archaeology. New discoveries are discussed during the tour to increase visitors' appreciation of Anasazi culture and civilization.

Professional guides explore the mysteries of the Anasazi and help visitors to appreciate the research involved in seeking the solutions to the still-unanswered questions: Who were they? How did they live? Where did they come from? Why did they leave? Where did they go?

Tours visit sites that are actually being excavated. Half-day and full-day tours are available; lunch is provided on all-day tours. Visitors ride in a fourteen-passenger van with a driver-host, and there are interpretive guides at each major stop on the tour.

Regular tours include Mesa Verde National Park, Hovenweep National Monument, Yellow Jacket, Crow Canyon Archaeological Center, Sand Canyon Pueblo, the Anasazi Heritage Center, the Escalante Ruin, and Lowry Ruin. And of course, en route to these archaeological destinations, the scenic splendor of the Four Corners area surrounds you!

All trips begin at the Cortez CU Center at 25 North Market in Cortez. Morning and all-day tours leave at 8:30 AM, and the second half-day trip leaves at 1:00 PM. Additional information on tours and other programs and events can be obtained at the Cortez CU Center or the Colorado Welcome Center/Cortez Area Chamber of Commerce. Inquiries may be addressed to the Cortez CU Center, P.O. Box 1326, Cortez, CO 81321. For more information or reservations call (303) 565-1151. Customized half-day and full-day tours are available, and pick-ups at campgrounds and motels can be arranged.

Cortez CU Center and Museum, 25 North Market Street, in the middle of downtown Cortez.

GUIDE TO CORTEZ FACILITIES

All Colorado telephone numbers in the Greater Cortez area are in the 303 area code.

LODGING AND FOOD

Motels

Anasazi Inn (AAA)
666 South Broadway
565-3773
Pool, restaurant

Aneth Lodge–Budget 6
645 East Main Street
565-3453

Arrow Motor Inn
440 South Broadway
565-3755
Pool, jacuzzi

Bell Rau Lodge (AAA)
2040 East Main, Highway 160
565-3738
Some kitchenettes, small outdoor pool

Best Western Sands Motor Inn (AAA)
1000 East Main
565-3761
Indoor pool, restaurant

Best Western Turquoise Motel (AAA)
535 East Main
565-3778
Outdoor pool, Pony Express Restaurant

Cortez Inn
2121 East Main, Highway 160
565-6000
Indoor jacuzzi and pool

El Capri
2110 South Broadway
565-3764
Pool, playground; German spoken

Far View Lodge
Mesa Verde National Park
529-4421
Only motel inside park; restaurant and gift shop

Frontier National 9 Inn
1920 East Main
565-3474
Jacuzzi, pool, family suites

Lazy G Motel
Highway 160 and 145
565-8577
Pool, restaurant, kitchens

Super 8 Motel
505 East Main
565-8888
Has four separate three bedroom apartment units with kitchenettes, washers, and dryers

Tomahawk Lodge (AAA)
810 South Broadway
565-8521
Pool

Travelers Motor Lodge
301 West Main
565-8562
Pool, jacuzzi, sundeck, Nero's Restaurant

Ute Mountain Motel
531 South Broadway
565-8507
Family suites

Bed and Breakfast

All Bed and Breakfast inns require advance reservations. The Cortez Area Chamber of Commerce in City Park can provide maps on how to reach them.

Kelly Place
14663 County Road G
Cortez, Colorado 81321
565-3123, 882-4943
A living history and archaeological preserve in the nation's Four Corners.

Simon Draw Guest House
13880 County Road 29
Cortez, Colorado 81321
565-8631
On the edge of a spectacular canyon view east of Cortez.

Restaurants

Anasazi Inn Apple Tree
666 South Broadway
565-3773
Family dining, breakfast, lunch, dinner

Antonio's
104 East Main
565-9066
Mexican food

Big Cheese Pizza
1438 East Main
565-6596
Lunch and dinner

Bob's Drive-in
610 North Broadway
565-3911
Fast food, lunch and dinner

Burger Boy Drive-in
400 East Main
565-7921
Fast food, lunch and dinner

El Grande Cafe
28 East Main
565-9996
Mexican and American food, breakfast and lunch until 5 PM

El Sombrero
2707 Mancos Road
565-4225
Mexican food

Francisca's Restaurant
125 East Main
565-4093
Mexican food, lunch and dinner

Golden Corral Family Steak House
1510 East Main
565-4703
Family dining

Homesteaders Restaurant
45 East Main
565-6253
Family dining, breakfast, lunch, dinner

Hong Kong Restaurant
1740 East Main
565-3719
Chinese, family dining

Hunan Chinese Restaurant
1100 East Main
565-9550
Family dining, adjacent to Best Western Sands Motel

Kentucky Fried Chicken
220 West Main
565-3863
Fast food

M and M Truck Stop
7006 Highway 160 and 666
intersection at Airport Road
565-6511

McDonalds
322 East Main
565-6004
Fast food, breakfast, lunch, dinner

Mr. T's
504 South Broadway
565-3152
Family dining, lunch and dinner

Nero's Italian Restaurant
303 West Main
565-7366
Dinner only, adjacent to Traveler's
Motel, outdoor patio in season

Pizza Hut
1119 East Main
565-4037
Lunch and dinner

Pippo's Coffee Bar
100 West Main
565-3066

Pony Express Restaurant
630 East Main
565-3475
Family dining, breakfast, lunch, dinner

Sonic Drive-in
436 South Broadway
565-3102
Fast food, lunch and dinner

Stromsted's Restaurant
1020 South Broadway
565-1257
Family dining, dinner only

Taco Time
332 West Main
565-7291
Fast Mexican food, lunch and dinner

Ute Coffee Shop
11 South Broadway
565-3621

**Warsaw Inn, Lazy G Motel and
Campground**
Junction of Highways 145 and 160
565-8585
Breakfast, lunch, dinner

BUSINESSES AND SERVICES

Airlines

Mesa Airlines
Montezuma County Airport (Cortez)
Nonstop service to and from Denver,
and connecting routes via
Farmington to Phoenix and
Albuquerque
800-545-5119 (Farmington)
800-637-2247 (reservations)

American West Airlines
La Plata County Airport (Durango)
800-247-5692
Connecting flights to Phoenix and the
West Coast

Continental Express
La Plata County Airport (Durango)
800-525-0280
Service to and from Denver

United Express
La Plata County Airport (Durango)
800-241-6522
Service to and from Denver, and
connecting routes via
Farmington

Automobile Dealers and Services

Ken's Pit Stop
720 South Broadway
565-4144

Marsell Motor Company
145 East Main
565-3418
Antique cars

Steve Keetch Motors Inc.
201 Pinon
565-3421
GM, Oldsmobile, Cadillac, Pontiac, Buick

Tom Redd Chevrolet
333 South Broadway
565-3748
Chevrolet, vans

Banks

Basin Industrial Bank
2 East Main
565-8565

Centennial Savings
343 East Main
565-3446

The Citizens State Bank of Cortez
77 West Main
565-8421

First National Bank
140 West Main
565-3781

Valley National Bank
350 West Montezuma
565-4411

Automatic Teller Location

Plus System
City Market Parking Lot
24-hour service

Bingo

Ute Mountain Ute Reservation
South of Cortez on Highway 666

Boat Dealers

Beaver Creek Marina
565-6114, 565-3412

Four Seasons Sports
28101 County Road, Dolores
882-4990

McPhee Marine
1638 East Main, Cortez
565-2628

Bookstores

Quality Book Store
34 West Main
565-9125
800-727-3081

The Book Nook
44 N. Ash Street
565-2010

Campgrounds and RV Facilities

Cortez Mesa Verde KOA Kampground
½ mile east on Highway 160
565-9301

Double A Campground
34979 Highway 160
565-3517

La Mesa RV Campground
1 Block west of Highway 160 and 145
2430 East Main
565-7156

Lazy G Motel and Campground
Highway 160 and 145
565-8577

Mesa Oasis Campground
5608 Highway 160-666 South
565-8716

Mesa Verde Kampark
35303 Highway 160
533-7421

Morfield Campground
Mesa Verde National Park
8 miles inside park, steep grade
565-4400

Williams Trailer Supply
641 South Broadway
565-9413

Camping Supplies

Handy Man South
806½ South Broadway
565-4301

Howard's Sporting Goods
16 West Main

Car Rentals

Hertz Auto Rental
Montezuma County Airport
565-8140

U Save Auto Rental
Montezuma County Airport or
920 South Broadway
565-9168

Contract Archaeologists (Cultural Resource Management Consultants)

Complete Archaeological Services Associates (CASA)
12400 Highway 666
565-9229

La Plata Archaeological Consultants
419 Central Avenue, Dolores
882-4933

Woods Canyon Archaeological Consultants
Yellow Jacket
562-4884

Laundromats

J and M Laundromat
831 East Main
565-4700

Wash 'N Clean World
605 Lakeside Commons
565-9202

Medical Facilities

Cortez Medical Clinic
33 North Elm
565-8556

Family Practice Associates
1021 North Mildred Road
565-4436

Southwest Memorial Hospital
1311 North Mildred Road
(one mile north of Colorado
    Welcome Center)
565-6666
565-7777 (Ambulance)
565-3448 (Poison Control)

Pharmacies/Drug Stores

City Market Pharmacy
508 East Main
565-6466

Professional Pharmacy
33 North Elm
565-7368 (day or night)

Revco Discount Drug Center
2214 East Main
565-7000

Walmart Pharmacy
2220 East Main
565-7038

Wilson Pharmacy
2 West Main
565-8558, 565-3022 (after hours)

Photographic Supplies

Cortez Camera
2830 East Main (Cortez Plaza)
565-4000
One hour color prints, film,
accessories.

Vic's Photo
112 West Main
565-7338

Taxidermy

Anderegg Taxidermy Service
Highway 160, ½ mile east of Cortez
565-4271

Trading Posts, Shops, and Galleries

Cliff Dweller Indian Arts and Crafts
1004 East Main
565-3424

Colorado Collectibles
30 West Main
565-4256

Cortez Silver and Gold
27762 Highway 160
565-4620

**Don Woodard's Indian
Trading Post Museum**
1 mile east of Cortez on Highway 160
565-3986

Four Winds Crafts and Antiques
48 West Main
565-1280

Indian Princess
30 East Main
565-2141

Ismay Trading Post
391 County Road G
565-7752

Little Bear
806 South Broadway
565-9372

Mesa Verde Pottery
27601 Highway 160
565-4492

Notah Dineh
309 North Broadway
565-9607 or 1-800-444-2024

The Pinon Tree
121 East Main
565-2497

Tava-Mawoosie
158 Highway 160
565-3534

Toh-Atin Gallery
27601 Highway 160
565-0105

Ute Mountain Pottery
Highway 666 south of Cortez
at Towaoc
565-8548

Travel Agencies

Care-free Travel
16 East Main
565-6464

Cortez Travel
9 West Main
1-800-441-4566 (outside
Montezuma County)
565-9295 (local)

Western Wear

IFA
10501 North Highway 666
565-3077

Nuway Western Wear
33 East Main
565-7673

Toggery
9 East Main
565-3167

RESOURCES AND RECREATION

Historical Societies

Montezuma County Historical Society

History enthusiasts will enjoy the Montezuma County Historical Museum in Cortez, located in the Montezuma County Annex Building at Montezuma and Chestnut Streets. It is open seasonally Wednesdays and Fridays from 2:00 to 4:00 PM.

Colorado Archaeological Society, Hisatsinom Chapter

Activity and membership information available at Cortez CU Center, Crow Canyon Archaeological Center, Anasazi Heritage Center, and Cortez Area Chamber of Commerce.

Swimming and Tennis

If you want to relax, there are many attractive local activities. The Cortez Municipal Pool is open seven days a week from May 28 through Labor Day, and is located in Cortez City Park along Highway 160 at Mildred Road. The telephone number is 565-7887.

The pool schedule is:
11:30 AM to 12:55 PM lap swim
1:00 to 5:00 PM open swim
5:00 to 7:00 PM family swim
Youth and adult fees are charged. The pool is located in twenty-nine acres of park near the Public Library (565-8117), with lighted tennis courts, and many picnic areas.

Golf

If you are a golfer, try the Cortez Municipal Golf Course (El Conquistador). The 18-hole course has a rating of Blue 70.8 and is the finest course on Colorado's western slope. It is located in northeast Cortez off Highway 145 and has a driving range, pro on duty, full pro shop, clubs and cart rental, snack bar, and lessons. Hours are 7:30 AM to dark seven days a week. The course is open year-round and is a popular cross-country skiing location during the winter. Numerous tournaments are planned every summer. Contact the pro shop for details; the number is 565-9208.

Events

Summer events include the Ute Mountain Rodeo in early June, the annual Arts and Crafts Fiesta in late June, the annual Superbowl of Fiddling Contest and the Cortez CU Center Invitational Art Show in early July, and the county fair in early August. Every Monday through Thursday evening from early June through Labor Day there are Native American dances in the City Park, adjacent to the Colorado Welcome Center.

TRAVEL TIPS FOR THE GREATER CORTEZ AREA

Some of the tours in this guide, or ones you may invent for yourself, require travel over all-weather, unpaved roads, and sudden rains may convert hard surfaces to mud holes. Even on paved routes, it is often a long distance between rural population centers, or even individual houses. A few words of advice will help you to enjoy your excursions!

Car Care   Make sure that your vehicle is in good working condition (mechanically sound, check tires and oil, etc.), that you start the day with a full tank of gasoline, and that you carry drinking water and other emergency supplies. If your car breaks down, stay with it—do not walk for help unless you are sure you are near a house or town.

The Environment   The combination of altitude and heat can make travel in the Four Corners area a physically exhausting experience if you are not prepared. Be sure to drink plenty of liquids and to carry water, juices, or other beverages with you. Many parks and monuments have signs warning of overexertion by persons with heart or other physical limitations—take these signs seriously. Hiking around open sites such as Hovenweep in the middle of the day during the summer is not a good idea.

Critters   Most crawling, slithering, and four-footed residents of the area will stay clear of you given the chance. In shady areas or less-visited regions, however, such as open countryside or in canyon bottoms beneath the cottonwood trees, you may encounter rattlesnakes. They will not bother you if you avoid them—*leave them alone and go on your way.*

It seems that every gnat that was ever born is either still living at Hovenweep or has gone back there to retire! They are particularly bad before the first heavy rains of the summer, although on some days the breezes will keep them at bay. Local archaeologists recommend Avon Products' "Skin-So-Soft" as the most effective repellent, despite its somewhat aromatic odor!

Respecting Native American (Indian) Peoples   The Four Corners region is still inhabited by a large, permanent population whose ancestors were living in the area thousands of years before Lief Ericson and Christopher Columbus "discovered" America. This is their home! Just as it would be offensive to have tourists come into your garden and take pictures of you while you are cooking out on the grill, these traditional residents of the region also deserve to have their lives, privacy, and activities respected. Except in a real emergency, wait to be recognized before approaching someone's house; ask before taking a picture, even in Cortez (unless it's a public performance where picture taking is encouraged as part of the program; expect to pay a modest camera fee). People may have better things to do than to answer your questions. And if, while hiking in the countryside, you come across small rock cairns, clusters of feathers, or other objects, *leave them alone.* The very fact that they are in out-of-the-way locales suggests they are religious shrine locations. Respect and do not disturb them.

Many archaeological sites in the Greater Cortez Area are unsupervised. *Please* do not deface or alter architecture, or pick up pottery or pretty rocks. Under no circumstances should you dig on public lands. The destruction of prehistoric resources is one of the greatest problems in the Four Corners area. The old adage, "take nothing but pictures, leave nothing but footprints," certainly applies!

Respecting Archaeological Remains

FALL SCENERY AND WINTER SPORTS IN THE GREATER CORTEZ AREA

Opportunities for great cross-country and downhill skiing, snowshoeing, snowmobiling, and ice fishing await the winter visitor to the Greater Cortez Area. Whether you trek through the pristine wilderness of the high Rockies, glide along the mesa tops where the ancient Anasazi Indians once lived, or traverse groomed slopes, exploring the Cortez area in winter gives new meaning to a Colorado winter vacation.

While the greatest number of tourists come to southwestern Colorado during the summer, the fall is an equally good time to experience the land of the Anasazi. In fact, the cooler fall weather and smaller crowds make certain trips much more pleasant. For example, Balcony House at Mesa Verde often has long lines during the summer, and from across the canyon the ladders at Cliff Palace appear to be covered by a stream of ants! In the fall, both of these features can be visited at a more leisurely pace.

Fall colors are also brilliant in the Four Corners area, and a late September drive from Durango to Cortez, or through Mesa Verde National Park, is an unforgettable experience. Later on in the fall, or early in the new year, Mesa Verde, Ute Mountain, the La Platas, the San Juans, and the Abajos are all draped in white and the bright reddish-oranges and purples of winter sunsets have to be seen to be believed and appreciated. The Colorado Welcome Center, Cortez Area Chamber of Commerce, Anasazi Heritage Center, and various national parks and monuments are open year round. Take advantage of the off season if your schedule permits.

Also, if you have the opportunity to visit Mesa Verde, Lowry, or other Anasazi sites during the winter, stop for a moment to contemplate (and appreciate) the adaptive skills of the inhabitants—no central heat, and no grocery stores to run to if their food supplies dwindled!

Cortez offers a change in climate that is much appreciated after a day of wintertime fun. The warm days and cool nights of the area are often a marked contrast to the extremes of the higher elevations. Also, the many fine restaurants and lodging facilities in the area offer rates to accommodate even the tightest budget. The city golf course is an excellent place to cross country ski!

San Juan National Forest

During times of new snowfall, virtually all roads in and around the San Juan National Forest are closed to vehicular traffic except Highway 145, running from Cortez north to Telluride, and roads running near the West Fork of the Dolores River.

In past seasons, one of the more popular areas for cross-country skiing and snowmobiling has been the Lizard Head Pass area, some fifty miles north of Cortez. This touring area is approximately 2,400 acres and is adjacent to the Lizard Head Wilderness Area. The area is rated good to excellent and trails offer varying degrees of difficulty.

McPhee Reservoir

Skiing around the McPhee Recreation Site (just ten miles north of Cortez) offers good conditions for the beginning to intermediate skier. Access to the area is from Highway 184, near the Anasazi Heritage Center. Ice fishing is permitted on McPhee Reservoir when conditions are favorable.

Areas within the San Juan National Forest suitable for cross-country skiing include such names as Boggy Draw, Turkey Flats, Burro Bridge, and Little Bean Canyon. All of these areas are within easy access of Cortez. For more information about conditions and maps for the San Juan National Forest and the McPhee Reservoir area, call the Dolores Ranger District at (303) 882-7296.

The entrance to the Telluride Ski Area is located seventy miles north of Cortez on Highway 145. The drive to Telluride, through the San Juan National Forest and over Lizard Head Pass, is one of the most spectacular in the world.

Telluride Ski Area

The Telluride ski area is located near the north base of Lizard Head Pass. Ski area trails are divided into 24 percent beginner, 50 percent intermediate, and 26 percent advanced/expert.

For more information about conditions and prices for the Telluride Ski Area, contact the Telluride Visitor Information Center, P.O. Box 653, Telluride, CO 81435, or call (303) 728-3041.

After significant snowfall, the superintendent of the park usually closes all or part of the Ruins Road for the winter. Visitors are allowed to ski, snowshoe, or hike the six-mile round trip road that encircles the Chapin Mesa.

Mesa Verde National Park

Fresh snow at Mesa Verde offers the best cross-country skiing conditions. Waxless skis are recommended. Winter visitors are encouraged to take advantage of the excellent view of the Cliff Palace ruin from across a canyon at a point north of the Sun Temple area. Cross-country skiers are reminded that unplowed roads are also popular for snowmobiles. Skiers need to be aware that they may not be alone in the woods—be alert for the wild creatures that make this area their home. As with any outdoor activity, skiers should always be aware of where they are, never ski alone, and respect private property.

For more information about conditions, write Mesa Verde National Park, CO 81330 or call the park offices at (303) 529-4475.

Ute Mountain Tribal Park also offers a wide variety of winter tours and cross-country trips. Call (303) 565-4684 for information and arrangements.

Ute Mountain Tribal Park

PART 2
ANCIENT TIMES AND MODERN RESEARCH

▼▼▼▼▼▼▼▼▼▼

Southwestern Colorado is on the boundary of the cultural and geographical region referred to as the Greater Southwest, which is often defined as extending from Las Vegas, New Mexico, to Las Vegas, Nevada, and from Durango, Colorado, to Durango, Mexico. For a more detailed discussion of the Anasazi, read Chapter Seven in E. Steve Cassells's *The Archaeology of Colorado* (Johnson Books, 1983), and, for a more in-depth treatment, Linda Cordell's *Prehistory of the Southwest.* (These and other books mentioned in the text are listed in Suggested Readings at the end of this volume).

History of Prehistoric Research in Southwestern Colorado

The prehistoric ruins of southwestern Colorado were first noted by Spanish explorers in the late eighteenth century, but serious exploration of the region did not begin until the latter quarter of the nineteenth century. The Wetherills discovered Cliff Palace, one of the most spectacular ruins at Mesa Verde, in December 1888. Their enthusiasm propelled them to further explorations in Mesa Verde and adjacent parts of the Four Corners region.

Stories of the mystique of the Mesa Verde cliff dwellings spread far and wide, and treks to the ruins became commonplace for adventurers such as Baron Gustaf von Nordenskiold, who visited in 1891. The Baron conducted excavations for a summer and acquired a large collection of ethnological specimens and prehistoric artifacts, all of which are now part of the collection of the Finnish National Museum in Helsinki; some of the collection is also in the Swedish National Museum in Stockholm, where it is now considered part of the Swedish National Treasure.

The creation of Mesa Verde National Park and the passage of a national antiquities protection law in 1906 slowly changed the nature of archaeological activity in the area. In much the same way that a group of the citizens of Durango attempted to prevent Baron von Nordenskiold from removing Mesa Verde artifacts late in the nineteenth century, many local residents still feel very protective of "their" ruins. It is encouraging that more and more residents of the Four Corners area are beginning to recognize the need to protect the prehistoric cultural resources for which the area is famous.

The Cortez CU Center, the Anasazi Heritage Center, the Crow Canyon Archaeological Center, the Montezuma Valley Historical Society, and the local chapter of the Colorado Archaeological Society are all helping to generate a positive public consciousness about the unique value of the area's prehistoric heritage. Visitors can maintain contact with the area and contribute to these efforts by becoming affiliated with any of these organizations.

At the beginning of the twentieth century, Dr. T. Mitchell Prudden, a medical doctor from Cambridge, Massachusetts, made an outstanding survey of the San

Earl H. Morris (1889-1956), early southwestern archaeologist who helped to establish the basis for future research in the Four Corners area. (University of Colorado Museum, Earl H. Morris Archives)

Juan drainage area. Traversing unknown territory by horse and buckboard with Native American guides, he visited and recorded many significant sites north of the San Juan River.

The University of Colorado has been involved in archaeological research in the Four Corners area since the second decade of the twentieth century, when Earl H. Morris began searching for evidence of the origins of the Anasazi (see *Among Ancient Ruins: The Legacy of Earl H. Morris*, a Johnson Books publication, 1986).

Following the early explorations by people such as the Wetherills and Baron von Nordenskiold, research at Mesa Verde progressed rapidly. Under the auspices of the newly formed National Park Service, Jesse Walter Fewkes worked in the park in 1908. Earl Morris began working there in 1913 and continued intermittent activity throughout his professional career, including major architectural consolidation and restoration projects. Since that time David Breternitz, Frank Eddy, Robert Lister, Jack Smith, and Joe Ben Wheat, all connected with the University of Colorado, have contributed to the growth of understanding about the Anasazi occupation of the Mesa Verde area.

University of Colorado students excavating at the Yellow Jacket Field School.

Paul S. Martin excavated the Lowry Ruin, north of Yellow Jacket, in 1938. Like Yellow Jacket, the main site has a Great Kiva and there are many smaller, "suburban" sites surrounding the larger central site. However, Lowry does not have the concentration of architectural remains

found at Yellow Jacket and other large sites such as Sand Canyon and Goodman Point. South and west of Yellow Jacket, just over the Utah border, is the headquarters of Hovenweep National Monument.

Starting in the early 1970s, David Breternitz directed one of the largest and perhaps the most successful archaeological mitigation projects ever supported by the United States government (Bureau of Land Management) in the Dolores River valley, which was to be dammed to impound the irrigation and recreation pool for the McPhee Reservoir. The results of this research are presented in exhibits at the Anasazi Heritage Center.

The University of Colorado has been excavating in the area near Yellow Jacket since 1953. The results of this research are presented in exhibits at the Cortez CU Center. Finally, the Crow Canyon Archaeological Center School has begun excavations at the large site of Sand Canyon and other sites in that area. Many prehistoric secrets remain to be carefully and scientifically revealed in the Four Corners area.

Prehistory of the Four Corners Area

The earliest Southwestern peoples, who may have been in the area as many as 10,000 years ago, shared general cultural traits with the rest of the New World's native peoples. It was only when people in the Four Corners area began to settle into semipermanent and permanent villages shortly after the beginning of the Christian era that the cultural patterns produced by the people that we identify as "Anasazi" began to appear. This is the name that modern people have applied to these prehistoric populations; we have no idea what they called themselves. Although not yet fully explored, the southwestern Colorado area is of great significance in understanding the development of Anasazi society.

The Anasazi occupied the Colorado Plateau from the first through the thirteenth century AD. Mesa Verde is perhaps the best-known site concentration in the northern Anasazi region and has a continuous occupation sequence from at least Basketmaker II (AD 200-400) through Pueblo III times (ca. AD 1300).

In the Greater Cortez Area, museum exhibits interpreting the developmental sequence of the Anasazi can be seen at the Cortez CU Center, the Anasazi Heritage Center, and Mesa Verde National Park.

*Chronological
chart of
southwestern
prehistory. (After
Lange, et al.
1988:4)*

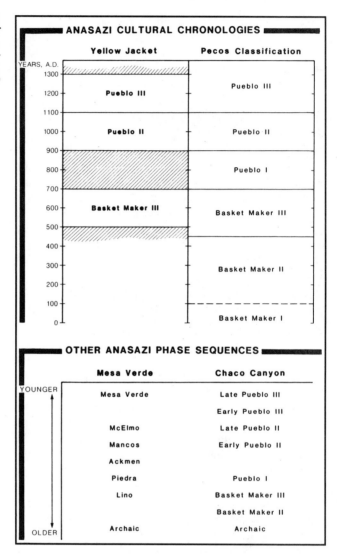

Chronological chart of southwestern prehistory. (After Lange, et al. 1988:4)

Minor chronological differences exist from site to site, and the dates given here may not be identical to those in use at Mesa Verde, Hovenweep, and other sites.

The following is a very brief overview of the broad outlines of prehistoric Anasazi cultural developments.

What About Basketmaker I?

The Four Corners archaeological sequence originally began with the Basketmaker I era, a hypothetical stage created originally to encompass the antecedents of the Anasazi. The term is no longer used, and archaeologists now use the term Archaic (5000 BC to AD 1) to refer to people who preceded the Anasazi.

Nomadic hunting groups began to settle and farm in the Southwest in this period. Three major sedentary culture groups arose: the Anasazi group focused in the Four

Basketmaker II:
AD 1-450

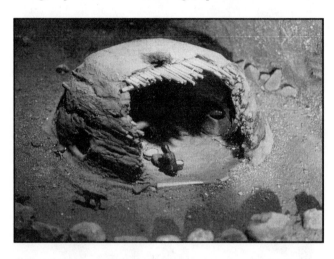

Basketmaker II house. (University of Colorado Museum diorama, Craig Hansen photograph)

Corners area, and the other two groups, the Hohokam and the Mogollon, centered mainly in Arizona.

The Anasazi grew crops such as corn and squash. Loincloths, belts, and sandals were worn in hot weather, and animal skins and fur or feather robes were added during the winter. Spears and atlatls (spear throwers) were used on the hunt. Projectile points were fashioned from a variety of materials including chert, chalcedony, and obsidian. Scrapers, axes, and other tools were essentially unchanged from earlier times. These people often lived in caves or constructed circular log homes. The term "basketmaker" refers to their well-constructed baskets that were used for portable containers, as pottery was not yet known.

Pithouses of wood and adobe were constructed as dwellings. A shallow, flattened, sometimes mud-plastered depression in the ground formed the floor. Walls of short log sections, laid crib style in mortar, were built to form the perimeter of the dwelling. Parallel poles were laid across the walls for roof supports and ceilings. The exterior was completely plastered with mud. A mano and metate (stone grinding tools), heating pit, and rock-lined storage bins were commonly found inside.

Basketmaker III:
AD 450-750

During this period populations grew. Trading with neighboring groups was more active. New ideas were adopted and traditions modified to meet changing needs.

Villages were composed of several pithouses and adjacent surface storage rooms. The developing agricultural society produced an increasing variety of tools. Animal bone was used to make awls, ornaments, and dice. The bow and arrow were introduced, and scrapers were used for thinning hides. Pottery was introduced and changed the cooking habits of the Basketmaker

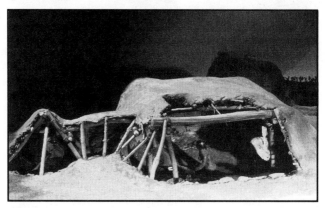

Basketmaker III house. (University of Colorado Museum diorama, Craig Hansen photograph)

people. These ceramic vessels could be used over fires and were waterproof.

Early Basketmaker III structures were supported by four or more vertical corner posts. Pithouses were dug deeper as the period progressed. There were now two rooms: the main living area and an antechamber. The rear part of the main room was used for living and sleeping, while the front served as a kitchen where women ground corn and prepared meals. A slab deflector protected the fire pit from drafts. A hatch in the roof served as ventilation and passageway. The pithouse roof was also part of the general living space.

Pueblo I:
AD 750-900

These people were originally thought to be of a different physical type because their skulls were flat in the back and generally rounder than those of the Basketmakers. We now know Basketmaker and Pueblo people to be the same genetically; the latter group had begun to strap their babies to hard cradleboards, which resulted in the cranial deformation.

Pottery decoration became more symmetrical and

Pueblo I house and village. (University of Colorado Museum diroama, Craig Hansen photograph)

controlled. Such changes reflected a continued development in community life and an increasing concern with religion and symbolism.

Dwelling changes were evident by AD 700. A few surface domestic rooms were added onto the rows of storage rooms. These structures, or pueblos, had storage spaces along the back. Each family had a living room and one or more storage rooms.

The pithouse was becoming the center of village social and ceremonial life and was evolving into a ceremonial chamber called a "kiva."

Pueblo II: AD 900-1050

Numerous sites in southwestern Colorado (Yellow Jacket, Sand Canyon, Lowry, Goodman Point, etc.), experienced significant population growth during Pueblo II times. Some sites, such as Yellow Jacket, began to evolve as regional centers.

Some animals, such as turkeys, were utilized for ceremonial purposes while others, such as rabbits, were not. We know that small game and large game were both important, suggesting that traps and snares were used as well as projectiles, and that women and children participated in hunting in addition to men.

In recent years, southwestern archaeologists increasingly have questioned the traditional interpretation of heavy reliance on maize agriculture by the Anasazi. The abundant natural resources in southwestern Colorado much more accurately indicate that a mixed subsistence economy was probably typical of the area.

The potters' art flourished. Distinctive forms and de-

*Pueblo II house
and village.
(University of
Colorado Museum
diorama,
Craig Hansen
photograph)*

signs now distinguished different regions. These regional variations within Pueblo culture were established
in little more than a century.

Surface rooms were now constructed of stone instead of poles and mud. Kivas increasingly were used
for ceremonial purposes. The first masonry buildings
were constructed during this period, along with the pole
and mud wall types. House-villages contained between
six and thirty rooms. Many of the small stone structures
built between AD 900 and AD 1050 became central cells
of larger pueblos. Pueblo II structures were sometimes
demolished by later builders in search of ready-cut
stones and timber.

Pueblo III:
AD **1050-1300**

Prehistoric regional centers such as Yellow Jacket,
Sand Canyon, and Mesa Verde are sites that had impor-
tance to people living in the area surrounding them.
They are generally larger than surrounding sites in the
same canyon or river valley, and normally there is only
one regional center in each major ecological niche.
While regional centers such as Pueblo Bonito in Chaco
Canyon (see Tour Route 4) have long been recognized
south of the San Juan River, little attention has been
paid to these regional centers north of the San Juan.

Yellow Jacket, Sand Canyon, and Goodman Point
are large Colorado sites with Great Kivas and no fewer
than seventy-five small kivas. No such sites exist south
of the San Juan drainage. Research at these unique sites
is essential to understanding Anasazi cultural development.

The Pueblo III, or Classic Pueblo period, was noted for strong local variation in arts and crafts. Many pueblos had become massive stone structures, often three or four stories in height. Larger kivas, or Great Kivas, were constructed fifty feet or more in diameter. The Classic Pueblo period represents the highest architectural achievement of Native Americans north of Mexico.

We do not yet fully understand the role of these regional centers. They may have been important because they were the centers for major religious ceremonies, or perhaps they had surpluses to distribute in case of crop failure. They may also have been focal points in regional and inter-regional trade networks, through which exotic goods such as obsidian or marine shells were made available to local residents. Administratively, they may have been similar to the county seats of historic times.

Pueblo III house and kiva complex. (University of Colorado Yellow Jacket excavation)

A gradual abandonment of the large pueblos was almost complete by the fourteenth century. Possible causes for this dispersion include extended droughts, over-exploited natural resources, internal conflicts, and perhaps, aggressive neighbors.

During prehistoric times this area was very rich in both plant and animal life. Rich upland soils supported extensive agriculture, and on the mesa tops, piñon, juniper, and sagebrush formed the main cover. In the canyon, there was a wide range of trees and smaller

Nature's Bounty and Impact

plants, including willow, oak, and various wild berries. In the marshy areas you could have found reeds, cattails, and other water-loving plants. Dogs and semi-domesticated turkeys were kept by the prehistoric inhabitants. Deer, antelope, beaver, porcupine, jackrabbits, cottontails, marmots, prairie dogs, ground squirrels, skunks, pocket gophers, bobcats, coyotes, sage hens, and the numerous wild turkeys provided an abundance of game. The inhabitants of this area were hunting, gathering, collecting, and horticultural groups. The environmental portions of the Dolores Archaeological Program model suggest that the history of the corn-growing Anasazi in the Four Corners area was closely tied to a dry farming belt that was continually in flux: it expanded, shrank, and sometimes disappeared altogether. Environmental shifts and stress are thought to have contributed to the abandonment of the area around AD 1300.

The prehistoric, historic, and natural richness of the Four Corners region and the Greater Cortez Area are highlighted in the countless combinations and variations of the nine tour routes presented in the following section.

PART 3
TOUR ROUTES

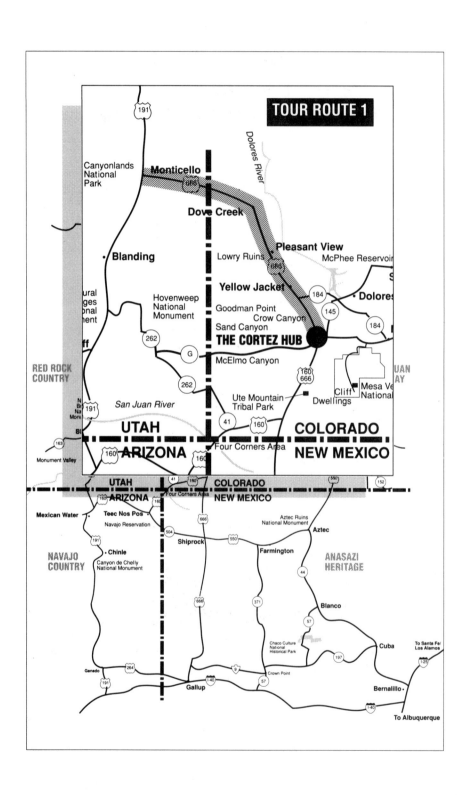

TOUR ROUTE 1
LARGE SITES OF SOUTHWESTERN COLORADO

▼▼▼▼▼▼▼▼▼

Little known and until recently ignored by southwestern archaeologists, there are perhaps a half dozen large sites in southwestern Colorado whose long-term preservation and study is a matter of paramount public interest and potential benefit. Those that are accessible to the public, either by private car or tour, are clustered along Tour Route 1.

One of the most striking characteristics of these sites is the large number of kivas relative to domestic rooms. Many have in excess of fifty or even one hundred kivas. Their high kiva/habitation ratio makes them distinctly different from anything known in the rest of the Southwest. Gaining an understanding of these sites will be one of the great challenges facing southwestern archaeology well into the twenty-first century.

Tour Route 1 can be combined with Tour Route 3 (preferably over a two-day period) to provide a comprehensive overview of Anasazi adaptation to the Four Corners area. Route 1 covers the rolling, relatively green uplands, while Route 3 crosses the more arid lowlands. The prehistoric Anasazi adapted their culture to both of these regions

CROW CANYON

Heading north from Cortez on Highway 666, the Crow Canyon Archaeological Center offers an educational experience for those who enjoy "hands-on" archaeology. Crow Canyon is unique in that it permits students and adults with no prior experience to participate in its research and education programs.

Crow Canyon Archaeological Research Center and Lodge.

Participants come from across the nation and from foreign countries to work with southwestern archaeologists and educators. They are currently excavating a variety of sites, including Sand Canyon, a vast thirteenth-century pueblo of more than 350 rooms, kivas, and towers. The research at Crow Canyon Archaeological Center will show you the full spectrum of scientific archaeology. At Sand Canyon Pueblo trained scientists and student archaeologists are uncovering the mysteries of one of the most significant sites in which the Anasazi lived.

Participants come in groups or individually. All participants work in one of the sites and in the newly constructed research laboratory and administrative center on campus. Lodging for participants is provided on the secluded and scenic Crow Canyon Archaeological Center campus, in comfortable shared quarters in the Crow Canyon Lodge, or the four-bed hogans. Modern shower and bath facilities are provided. The kitchen provides three meals per day, and the menu is varied and plentiful. To register, call Crow Canyon Archaeological Center toll-free at 1-800-422-8975. Make your reservations early; many weeks fill quickly. For local information, call (303) 565-8975 or write Crow Canyon Archaeological Center, 23390 Road K, Cortez, CO 81321. Some evening lectures are open to the public and are announced in local news media.

Excavations at Sand Canyon, Crow Canyon Archaeological Center.

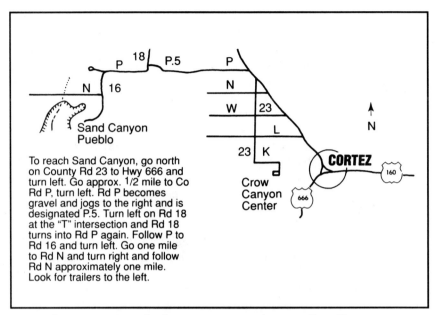

To reach Sand Canyon, go north on County Rd 23 to Hwy 666 and turn left. Go approx. 1/2 mile to Co Rd P, turn left. Rd P becomes gravel and jogs to the right and is designated P.5. Turn left on Rd 18 at the "T" intersection and Rd 18 turns into Rd P again. Follow P to Rd 16 and turn left. Go one mile to Rd N and turn right and follow Rd N approximately one mile. Look for trailers to the left.

SAND CANYON

Sand Canyon is reached via County Road P, an all-weather road. The above map should lead you directly to the site, where there is a self-guided tour.

GOODMAN POINT

This is another large, multi-kiva and room-block ruin administered by Mesa Verde National Park. The site is unexcavated and there are no permanent interpretive facilities. It is impressive in its dimensions and canyon-head setting. This site can be reached via County Road P (see the Sand Canyon map). Be careful of climbing on architectural features and treat the site with respect. As you cross the site, you will notice a cluster of cattails at the head of a slickrock area dropping off into the canyon. The cattail stands, indicative of moisture retention in the soil, are common features at all the large, high-frequency kiva sites in southwestern Colorado. There is also a Great Kiva at Goodman Point.

YELLOW JACKET

In the late nineteenth century, the stage line from Dolores, Colorado, to Monticello, Utah, crossed the drainage of Yellow Jacket Creek. A stage stop was established near a spring where an abundance of local "stingers" gave the name Yellow Jacket to local geographical nomenclature. Little did the stage passengers know that they were passing by one of the most significant concentrations of prehistoric sites in the Southwest!

Just south of where Highway 666 crosses Yellow Jacket Creek, headward erosion has cut a deep canyon containing the permanent spring-fed stream that attracted prehistoric peoples and the early stage stop. At this point, another creek from the north joins Yellow Jacket Creek, leaving a flat point of land nearly a mile long and several hundred feet wide between the two. A nearly continuous series of ruins collectively known as the Yellow Jacket ruin cover this peninsula. This large site cluster must have been a prehistoric regional center, as it contains one Great Kiva, five intermediate-size kivas, 124 small kivas, multistoried buildings, towers, and indications of almost continuous occupation from about AD 500 to 1300.

After turning off at Yellow Jacket, the sight greeting the visitor is the landmark facade of the Yellow Jacket Store and Post Office. As of 1989, one could still mail letters here (with a hand-cancelled postmark!), although the store is no longer in business. One contract archae-

Yellow Jacket Store and Post Office

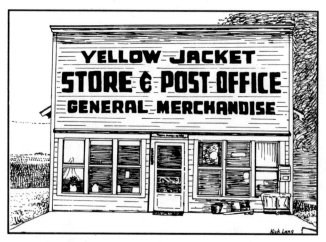

ology firm in Cortez mails all of its business correspondence from this post office. On a cold morning, the warmth from the pot belly stove is a welcome friend.

The sites at Yellow Jacket are all on private property and can be visited only by prior arrangement. Anasazi Tours in Cortez conducts some tours during the summer; because of road conditions, the sites are inaccessible during the winter and spring. If you know where to stop and look along Highway 666, just south of the Yellow Jacket turn-off, you can look out across the broad expanse of the site any time of the year.

The most striking impression one acquires of the Yellow Jacket area is the extreme complexity of the pre-historic remains, brought about by repeated rebuilding on the same sites for many centuries. The Anasazi must have felt very at home here! A more detailed description of the work at Yellow Jacket can be found in *Yellow Jacket: A Four Corners Ceremonial Center* (Johnson Books, 1988).

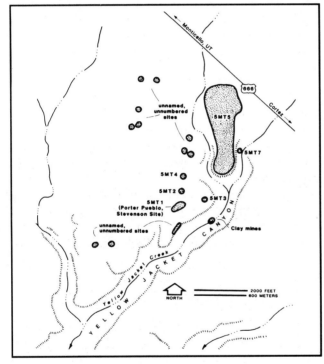

Map of Yellow Jacket archaeological complex. (After Lange, et al. 1988: 13)

The Lowry Ruins are north of Yellow Jacket, a short drive off Highway 666, on a gravel road west of Pleasant View. There are access roads both south and north of Pleasant View. Watch for the signs and follow the all-weather road. During the agricultural season, be alert for large tractors and hay wagons. As you drive along, enjoy the vistas of the surrounding area and the contrasts between the red soil and the green-yellow crops. Lowry is a many-room pueblo built on the top of the plateau, and a kiva has been reconstructed inside. You may enter the kiva and see the remains of painted plas-

LOWRY RUINS

ter on the walls, although it has deteriorated significantly since excavation.

Lowry is managed by the Bureau of Land Management and has covered and numbered interpretive signs. It was constructed about AD 1090 by Anasazi farmers who raised corn, beans, and squash and also hunted. A community of perhaps one hundred persons lived here. Southeast of the reconstructed portion of the site is one of the largest Great Kivas, or ceremonial chambers, ever found. Following the signs, it is possible to drive from Lowry Ruins to Hovenweep National Monument without returning to Cortez.

Forgotten essential supplies before leaving Cortez? Need to gas up or get a cold bottle of pop on the way back to town? The Arriola Store at the corner of County Road South and Highway 666, the Dawson Lake and Round-Up stores at the intersection of Highway 666 and Highway 184, the Farmer's Co-op just south of the Yellow Jacket turn-off, and stores in Pleasant View and Dove Creek all have a selection of camping and fishing supplies, cold drinks, gasoline, groceries, and pay telephones. Some of these stores are closed on Sundays, and their evening closing hours may vary. Stopping at these smaller stores and post offices provides an opportunity to meet some friendly, helpful local residents who know more about fishing and road conditions than anyone. Think of yourself as the Charles Kuralt of the Four Corners area!

DOVE CREEK

From this small community, scenic vistas expand in every direction. For a spectacular overview of the Dolores River and canyon, stop at the Dolores River Overlook.

FACILITIES   All telephone numbers use the 303 area code.

Motels and Restaurants

Budget 6 Motel
418 West Highway 666
667-2234
Restaurant next door

Blue Mountain Cafe
580 West Highway 666
677-2261

Western Cafe
West Highway 666
677-2245

OTHER ATTRACTIONS AND SERVICES

Dove Creek is the "Pinto Bean Capital of the World," and warehouses and processing plants line Highway 666. Dove Creek is also the home of the high-altitude gourmet Anasazi Bean, a distinctive red and white bean that is increasingly available commercially. Large bulk bags of beans, or one-pound souvenir sizes in brightly decorated burlap bags, are available throughout southwestern Colorado. Bookstores carry a variety of pinto bean cookbooks with directions for a wide range of delicacies, including pinto bean chocolate cake!

Groceries and camping and automotive supplies are also available in Dove Creek.

MONTICELLO

On the edge of the Abajos, or Blue Mountains, Monticello, Utah, offers an exhilarating collection of views and scenery. During the winter it is the gateway to skiing, snowmobiling, and other winter sports in the nearby mountains. Restaurants, groceries, camping and automotive supplies are also available.

FACILITIES   All telephone numbers use the 303 area code.

Motels and Hotels

Best Western Wayside Inn
197 East Central
587-2261

Canyonlands 6 Motel–Five Star Friendship Inn
197 East Main
587-2266

Grist Mill Inn Bed and Breakfast
64 South 3rd East
587-2597

Navajo Trail Motel
248 North Main
587-2251

Triangle H Motel
164 East Highway 666
587-2274

Campgrounds and RV Parks

Buckboard National Forest
6.5 miles off Highway 191

Dalton Springs National Forest
5 miles west off Highway 191

KOA Monticello
5 miles east on Highway 666
587-2884

Mountain View Camper Park
632 North Main
587-2974

Newspaper Rock State Park
12 miles off Highway 191 on Highway 211

Rowley's Trailer Park
480 North Main
587-2355

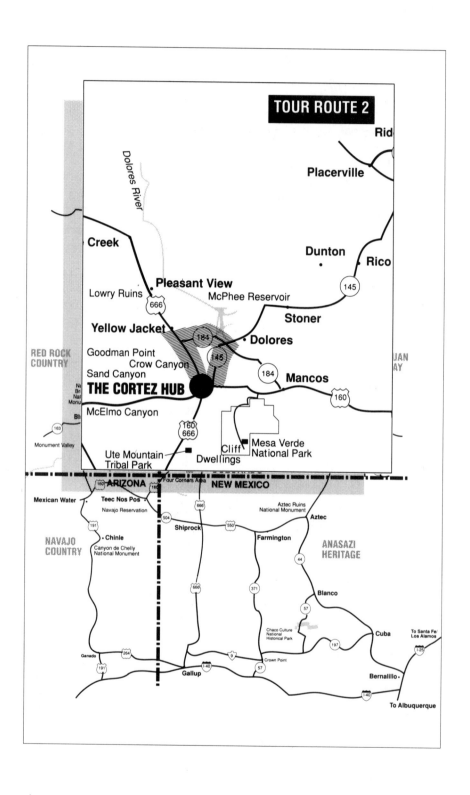

TOUR ROUTE 2
ANASAZI HERITAGE CENTER,
McPHEE RESERVOIR, AND DOLORES

▼▼▼▼▼▼▼▼▼

The Anasazi Heritage Center is an important educational facility that interprets the results of the Dolores Archaeological Program and southwestern prehistory. The museum and research center can be reached by turning west off Highway 145 onto Highway 184 about one mile south of Dolores, or by turning right onto Highway 184 at the Dawson Lake Corner on Highway 666 north of Cortez.

The Anasazi Heritage Center is a pueblo-style building set on a hillside, with a curved southern facade to take advantage of both beautiful views and abundant solar energy. Hours are 9:00 AM to 5:00 PM. Monday through Saturday and 10:00 AM to 5:00 PM Sunday. The goal is to make the museum fun as well as educational. The Heritage Center exhibits teach visitors about the Anasazi's relationship to the environment. They also educate visitors and local people on historic preservation. The lobby has a souvenir and book sales area. For further information, write the Center at 27501 Highway 184, Dolores, CO 81323, or call (303) 882-4811.

Anasazi Heritage Center, McPhee Reservoir

The main exhibit hall tours are self-guided. Life-size cutout figures of an Anasazi family, complete with pet dog and turkey, greet visitors. Exhibits show how the Anasazi farmed, made ceramics, and lived. A reconstructed pithouse is an authentic tableau of the daily life of the Anasazi in AD 800. Exhibits also show modern archaeologists working and explain the management and conservation of cultural resources, especially demonstrating how citizens can help to prevent vandalism of irreplaceable sites.

An exciting feature is a hands-on Discovery Area, for children and adults. One exercise involves matching tree rings to tell the exact age of a beam from an Anasazi structure. Visitors can grind corn on a metate to see how difficult it is; other experiences include weaving, computer games dealing with archaeology, and microscopes to view samples of plants used by the Anasazi. Heritage Center staff are available in the Discovery Area to assist visitors.

Twelfth-century Anasazi ruins are nearby. The Dominguez Ruin can be seen along the path to the entrance of the Heritage Center and the Escalante Ruin is a short walk up the hillside along a well-marked trail.

McPHEE RECREATION AREA

While the Heritage Center focuses on the past, the nearby McPhee Recreation Area holds plenty of excitement for the present. Fishing on McPhee Reservoir is getting better every year and rave reviews keep pouring in. Fishing enthusiasts are becoming hooked on McPhee! According to Mike Japhet, a fishery biologist with the Colorado Division of Wildlife, "There are very few lakes in Colorado where rainbow trout and crappies can be caught in abundance, but McPhee Reservoir can claim this distinction." Large-mouth and small-mouth bass are also found in these waters.

McPhee Reservoir has 4,470 surface acres and is the second largest lake in Colorado. There are more than fifty miles of shoreline and several long, narrow tree-lined canyons. Maximum water depth at the dam is 270 feet. Underwater havens such as flooded trees, brush, and rock piles are attractive to fish. Through 1988, McPhee has been stocked with almost three million fish, and the Division of Wildlife plans to add at least another half million trout each year.

McPhee Reservoir is easy to reach, next to State Highways 145 and 184. Two major recreation sites with boat ramps and five fishing access points make getting there easy. There is a modern fish-cleaning station at the McPhee Recreation Site that simplifies the process of getting your fish ready to eat.

Water Sports at McPhee

There are water sports for everyone! Many people enjoy boating, and McPhee makes it more convenient with two boat ramps. Boat ramps are also available at nearby Narraguinnep Reservoir and Totten Lake. Water skiing is popular at all three locations. In addition, the five fishing access points around the reservoir are on

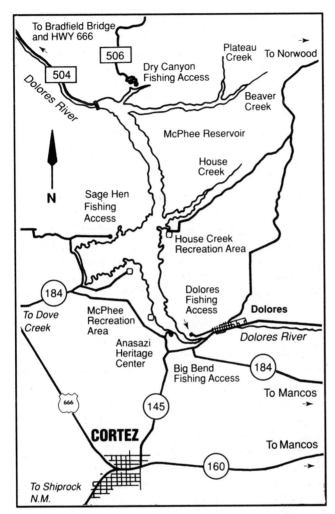

improved gravel or paved roads. All have parking and some have toilets and boat launching sites.

The Dolores access can be reached from the town· of Dolores. Go straight west on Central Avenue, which is the old river road on the north side of the reservoir. The road ends at the water, sloping gradually. Boats on trailers may have trouble putting in.

The new Dolores Town Park access is another popular spot for people who fish. Parking and flush toilets are provided. The Big Bend access is located off Highway 184, about half a mile west of Highway 145. Boats can put in here.

The Old McPhee County Road 27 access is reached off Highway 145. Boats can be put in here.

The Sage Hen County Road X access is on the west side of McPhee. Turn off Highway 184 at the signs for McPhee Recreation Area. Boats can be put in here and vault toilets are provided..

At the McPhee Recreation Site on the west side of the reservoir is a six-lane concrete boat ramp, with parking for 115 cars and 98 boat trailers. The House Creek boat ramp on the east side of the lake has a four-lane

Water sports at
McPhee Reservoir

concrete boat ramp that gets you into the water quickly
and easily. Parking for 85 cars and 75 boat trailers is
provided. Boats can be rented at Outfitter Sporting
Goods in Dolores and at McPhee Marine in Cortez.

Motorboats are not the only ones using McPhee.
With a steady summer southwest wind, sailboats are
also popular. Houseboats are welcome, although there
is a fourteen-day limit to discourage taking up permanent residence! This is always a danger when visitors
discover the natural beauty, prehistoric attraction, and
extensive facilities in the Greater Cortez Area. Wakeless
zones have been established at the mouth of the House
Creek area, the Dry Canyon arm, and two miles up the
Beaver Creek arm. This protects still-water fishing, and
creates a good location for canoes, rowboats, and rafts.

Newer water sports, including sail boards and jet
skis, also provide a means to cool off. Equipment can
be rented at Four Seasons Sports on Highway 145 one
mile south of Dolores. Four Seasons Sports also has a
certified boat mechanic on duty.

Boaters need to exercise caution for floating debris,
common in a fluctuating reservoir and particularly in a
new reservoir. A copy of Colorado boating regulations
can be obtained when a boat is purchased or registered.
The Montezuma County Sheriff's Department enforces
state statutes, including vessel operation and registra-
tion, and will make spot checks. Division of Wildlife pa-
trols enforce fishing and wildlife regulations, and the
Forest Service administers recreation and reservoir rules,
such as the wakeless zones.

The Galloping Goose Train

The Galloping Goose was an ingenious gasoline-
powered railroad bus invented to save the narrow
gauge Rio Grande Southern Railroad from going out of
business. The body of an old Buick automobile was the
cab for the motorman and coach for the passengers.
Mail and express were carried in the baggage car, a re-
inforced box-like structure mounted onto the cab. From
1931 to 1952, seven such conveyances galloped along
the railroad line that passed through Dolores, Rico, and
Telluride. Goose No. 5 now sits in Flanders Park at Dolores Town Hall, Fourth and Highway 145, and is a popular photo stop. These "railroad buses" replaced passenger trains on the local routes and temporarily saved the

railroad by giving faster and better service than steam locomotives. By the 1940s improved highways favored the trucking industry over the railroads.

DOLORES   The Dolores River gave its name to the town, and continues to provide water, lush green summer pastures, recreation, and the source of McPhee Reservoir. The full Spanish name, "Rio de Nuestra Señora de las Dolores," means "River of Our Lady of Sorrows." One legend recounts that it was named because an early explorer drowned there, while another is that the sound of the rushing water sounded sorrowful to the early explorers. Yet a third explanation is that early Spanish Catholic explorers named it Dolores for religious reasons. The town is about 7,000 feet in elevation.

The first settlement in 1877 was at Big Bend, about one and a half miles downstream. Here the Dolores River proves its uniqueness: it is the only river in North America to flow first south, then north! Big Bend was abandoned in 1891, when the Rio Grande Southern Railroad bypassed the settlement. The people moved next to the new tracks at the present townsite of Dolores.

Today ranching, farming, mining, logging, oil and gas, and tourism support the population of about 1,000. Besides the McPhee Reservoir, visitors are drawn to the camping, fishing, and hunting in the San Juan National Forest adjacent to Dolores. Whitewater rafting is becoming increasingly popular in this area; see Tour Route 9 for information on rafting the Dolores River.

The annual celebration of Escalante Day is the second Saturday in August. The day's events include a parade, games and contests for children and adults, and food and crafts booths in the park at 4th and Railroad.

Pleasant's Old West Antiques at Fourth and Central in Dolores features a museum, specializing in old printing equipment. Owner Larry Pleasant was a printer for fifty years. The Village Blacksmith at 11th Street and Highway 145 features one of the few remaining working blacksmiths in the country. Handcrafted gifts are offered for sale.

Picnicking and playgrounds for the kids are available just north of City Park in the new Centennial Park. The Dolores Road Park off Highway 145 in northeast Cortez is also popular.

The Dolores Chamber of Commerce can be reached by telephone at either (303) 882-7714 or (303) 882-4486 and is located at 211 Railroad Avenue in Dolores. The Chamber can provide extensive information on Dolores facilities.

FACILITIES   All telephone numbers use the 303 area code.

Motels and Hotels

Dolores Mountain Inn
Highway 145
882-7203

Outpost Motel and RV Park
East edge of Dolores on Highway 145
882-7271

Remuda Inn
1121 Central Avenue
882-4633

Rio Grande Southern Hotel and Restaurant
On the Town Square
882-7527

Stoner Lodge
25134 Highway 145, fourteen miles east of Dolores on road to Rico and Telluride
882-7825

Restaurants

The Depot
520 Railroad Avenue, Highway 145
882-7500

Dolores River Line Camp
Ranch Style Meals and Western Show
9 miles upriver from Dolores on
Highway 145
882-4148 (call for reservations)

Old Germany Restaurant
Highway 145 and 8th Street
882-7549

Ponderosa Restaurant
Highway 145 and 8th Street
882-7910

Sandwich Works, Inc.
Corner of Second and Railroad Avenue
(Highway 145)

Markets and Supplies

Dolores Food Market
509 Central
882-4792

The Whiskey Drummer
100 South 4th
882-4792

Campgrounds and RV Parks

Dolores RV Park
18680 Highway 145 (two miles
east of Dolores)
882-7761

Outpost Motel and RV Park
East edge of Dolores
on Highway 145
882-7271

**Ground Hog Fishing Camp
and Outfitters**
32 miles north of Dolores via Dolores
Norwood Road
882-4379

Recreational Equipment

Four Seasons Sports
Two miles west of Dolores
882-4990

The Outfitter (Sporting Goods)
410 Railroad Avenue (Highway 145)
882-7740

Humpback Chub River Tours
24588 Highway 145
882-7745

Sportsman Center
½ mile east of Dolores on Highway 145
882-7821

Shops and Galleries

Generic Jeans Factory Outlet
6th and Highway 145
882-7482

Unique Boutique
1320 Railroad Ave (Highway 145)
882-7745

Pleasant's Old West Antiques
4th and Central
882-7911

**West Fork Gallery and Custom
Frames**
105 South 5th Street
882-7688

**Rainbow Pharmacy and
Soda Fountain**
501 Central Avenue
882-7333

Other Services

Bud's Auto Repair
17631 Highway 145
882-7742

San Juan Taxidermy
4th and Railroad
882-7515

Dolores Coin-Op Laundry
310 Railroad

TOUR ROUTE 3
HOVENWEEP, MCELMO CANYON, BLUFF, AND BLANDING

▼▼▼▼▼▼▼▼▼▼

This route is most rewarding as an all-day trip. The route goes west from Cortez through the spectacular red rock beauty of McElmo Canyon. Preserved Anasazi Indian ruins, over 700 years old, can be visited and explored both at the Hovenweep Square Tower Ruins and at Lowry Ruins. A sense of the relationship the Anasazi had with the land is one result of seeing the locations of their former settlements in this very arid environment. During the summer this area is extremely hot and visitors should either avoid hiking during midday or be sure to carry water and take frequent rests in the shade.

Tour Route 3 can be combined with Tour Route 1 (over a two-day period) to provide a comprehensive overview of Anasazi adaptation to the Four Corners area. Route 1 covers the rolling, relatively green uplands, while Route 3 crosses the more arid lowlands. In these diverse environments the prehistoric Anasazi adapted and developed their culture.

Battle Rock

A battle between the Utes and Navajos gave this rock its name. As the battle progressed, the Navajos lost ground to the Utes. The Utes had a superior force and the Navajos made their last stand on top of the rock, reportedly jumping to their deaths rather than surrendering. Battle Rock is located about eleven miles west of Montezuma County Airport on the McElmo Canyon Road (County Road G). Battle Rock School is one of the few surviving one-room schoolhouses in the United States with grades K-6. The students are children of the residents of McElmo Canyon.

McElmo Canyon

As you proceed west, the road will change from pavement to all-weather, and you will soon drop down into the lush bottoms of McElmo Canyon. The large farms and ranches were first developed in the nineteenth century and are still important. The stone houses and school are vestiges of Mormon history in McElmo Canyon. The Kelly Place Bed and Breakfast and educational research facility is located on the north side of this road. Ask at the Cortez Chamber of Commerce for specific directions.

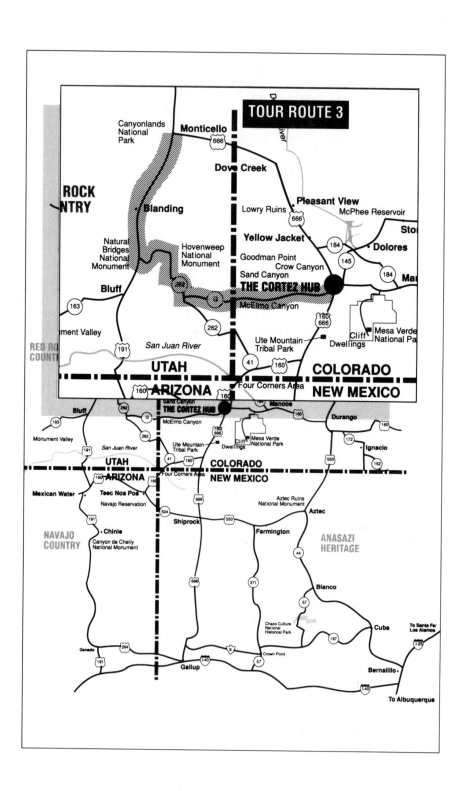

As you go farther west and approach the open end of the canyon, the land becomes more arid, until you are once again in semidesert. Just before crossing McElmo Wash, you will come to Ismay's Trading Post, marked by a huge pile of glass bottles. The trading post has faded from its former glory, but some pawn jewelry, Navajo blankets, and Ute beadwork are still found in the store. A cold can of pop never tasted better on a hot summer's day.

At the Aneth turn off, take a right and you regain the pavement, following it around until it forms a T near a large water tank; the right fork leads to Hovenweep National Monument. If you proceed straight on the pavement, you will drop down and cross through some fantastic geological features and painted landscape, eventually arriving at Hatch's Trading Post. Like Ismay's, it is no longer the hub of activity it once was, but still carries some native crafts and basic supplies. The deep shade is most welcome on a hot summer's day, and yes, those are peacocks that you see strutting around! The pavement continues to the left and is the civilized way to go to Blanding, Utah; the right fork goes back to dirt and proceeds up through Montezuma Creek Canyon to Blanding. The time difference between the dirt road and the pavement can be as much as two hours depending on conditions. The nearest overnight accommodations are at Blanding and Bluff in Utah and Cortez in Colorado.

Hovenweep National Monument

"Hovenweep" is a Ute Indian word that means "deserted valley." In addition to the main monument area, outlying archaeological sites include Horseshoe Ruins, Hackberry Ruins, Holly Ruins, Cajon Ruins, and Cutthroat Castle Ruins. The roads to these outlying sites are mostly dirt that turns quickly to adhesive-like mud during summer rains. Current conditions and maps should be obtained from the park ranger office before trying to reach these sites. There is no entrance fee to any of the Hovenweep ruins. Please be especially careful with the prehistoric and natural resources in these fragile areas.

The first report of ruins in the Hovenweep area was by W.D. Huntington, the leader of a Mormon expedition to present southeast Utah in 1854. The name was given by the famous pioneer photographer William H. Jackson, who visited the ruins in 1874. Dr. J.W. Fewkes of the Smithsonian Institution made an archaeological survey of the ruins in 1917-18 and recommended that they be protected as a national monument.

Tower structure, Hovenweep National Monument

There were contacts between the Anasazi who lived at Mesa Verde and the Anasazi who lived at Hovenweep. However, the type of villages varied greatly according to the environmental settings. A most distinctive feature of the Anasazi living at Hovenweep are the towers. These towers are often described as defensive, but this probably was not the case. Exactly how they were utilized awaits further research at Hovenweep and at other sites. The descendants of the prehistoric inhabitants of Hovenweep are probably the present-day Pueblo Indians of New Mexico and Arizona.

Many archaeologists and astronomers believe that three buildings at Hovenweep reflect a widespread knowledge of celestial events by the Native Americans. These buildings contain features that mark the summer solstice on June 21, winter solstice on December 21, vernal equinox on March 21, and autumnal equinox on September 21. For more information on this subject, read J. McKim Malville's *Prehistoric Astronomy in the Southwest.*

Near the monument headquarters, a self-guiding trail leads through the prehistoric ruins of Square Tower Group, around the head of the canyon and down into the canyon bottom. A park ranger is on duty all year to assist you with more information.

There is a modern thirty-one-site campground with restrooms, drinking water, picnic tables, and cooking grills. This is a U.S. fee area and the campground cost is $3 per night. Bring your own firewood or charcoal.

BLUFF

Bluff is southwestern Utah's oldest historic community, having been settled by the 250 Mormon settlers who came over the Hole in the Rock trail during the winter of 1879-80. Many of their original sandstone houses are still standing.

FACILITIES   All telephone numbers use the 801 area code.

Motels and Hotels

Bluff Bed and Breakfast
672-2220

Recapture Lodge
672-2281

Mokee Motel
672-2217

Scorup Bed and Breakfast
672-2272

Campgrounds and RV Parks

Turquoise RV Park
Highway 191
672-2219

Sand Island (BLM)
3 miles west on San Juan River

Other Services

Restaurants, groceries, camping, and automotive supplies are also available.

BLANDING

Blanding is a picturesque community halfway between Monticello and Bluff on Highway 191. It is the gateway to numerous scenic and winter/summer recreational areas in southeastern Utah, including the Manti-La Sal National Forest.

FACILITIES   All telephone numbers use the 801 area code.

Motels and Hotels

Best Western Gateway Motel
88 East Center
1-800-678-2278

Cliff Palace Motel
132 South Main
676-3231

Old Hotel Bed and Breakfast
164 East 200
678-2388

Prospector Motor Lodge
South Highway 191
678-3231

Campgrounds and RV Parks

Kampark
South Highway 191
678-2770

Devil's Canyon National Forest
9.5 miles northeast of Blanding on Highway 191

Museums

Edge of the Cedars Museum
The Edge of the Cedars State Historical Monument is the site of an Anasazi ruin and modern museum complex operated by the Utah Division of Parks and Recreation. The museum features exhibit halls, an auditorium, meeting and conference facilities, and a Native American arts and crafts shop. The history of San Juan County, from the ancient Anasazi through the Navajo and Ute Indians and Euro-American settlers, is represented. The museum also has one of the largest interpreted Anasazi pottery collections in the Southwest. Educational programs involve participation in the excavation program at the adjacent ruin. The museum and monument are located on the northwest edge of Blanding and are easily accessible by following the directional signs through town. Telephone: (801) 678-2238.

Other Services

Restaurants, groceries, camping, and automotive supplies are also available.

The next larger community north of Blanding is Monticello, Utah. A directory of Monticello facilities is included in the section on Tour Route 1. For additional information on Canyonlands and southeastern Utah, call 1-800-635-MOAB.

TOUR ROUTE 4
NAVAJO AND HOPI GATEWAY

▼▼▼▼▼▼▼▼

From the north and east, Cortez is also the gateway to the Navajo and Hopi Reservations and their natural and cultural attractions. Each of these areas is really a focus by itself and not a side trip from somewhere else. As a gateway, Cortez can point you in the right direction, and this section is designed to whet your appetite!

Before you start across the Navajo Reservation, please remember that the sale, purchase, or possession of any kind of alcoholic beverage is illegal on the reservation. Navajo tribal police have the authority to patrol the highways and roads that cross the reservation and it is not unusual to encounter spot checks.

Navajo Reservation Day Trip

The path to the Navajo Reservation begins on the south side of Cortez. Follow Highway 666 south, past the Ute Mountain Pottery plant, to the intersection with Highway 160 west. Turn west and head in the direction of Flagstaff and the Grand Canyon. Very shortly you will come to the Four Corners Monument, which is well worth seeing despite its touristy appearance! There is a small visitor orientation area. Numerous booths sell food, jewelry, and other souvenirs. Quality varies from booth to booth, and the knowledgeable buyer can occasionally get a real bargain.

When you leave the Four Corners Monument, turn right and proceed west on Highway 160. Shortly you will come to Teec Nos Pos, where Highway 160 intersects Highway 504. There is an excellent trading post on this corner and it is worth stopping in. After you have stopped, turn right and keep going west on Highway 160. Mexican Water is a good place to stop, fill up with gas, and have a cold drink or cup of coffee. Just beyond the trading post and gas station, Highway 191 turns south from Highway 160.

If you proceed west on Highway 160, you will go through Kayenta (which has all services and accommodations) and on to Navajo National Monument, with the spectacular ruins of Keet Seel and Betatakin, and campgrounds and visitors center. The drive will also give you a close-up view of the gigantic Black Mesa Coal Mining Project.

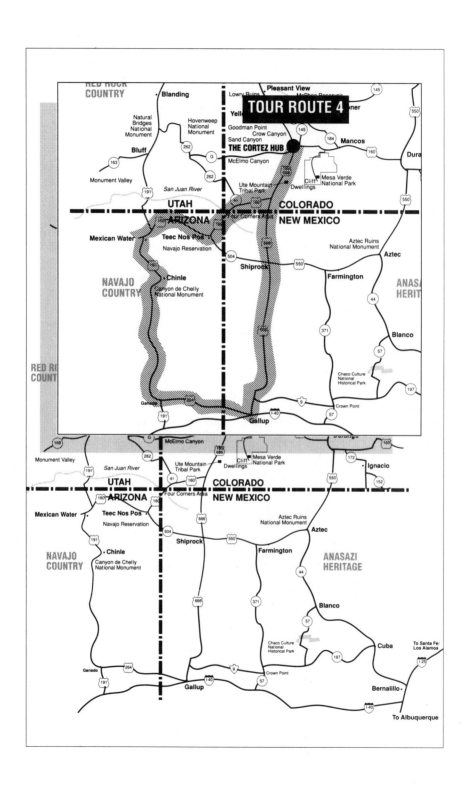

Near Navajo National Monument, the Shonto Trading Post is located deep in a canyon bottom. The picturesque setting is full of cottonwood shade, and the trader usually has a good supply of Navajo blankets, baskets, and pottery in the back room. Ask to see them. The post closes over the noon hour.

Proceeding westward on Highway 160 from Navajo National Monument, one eventually arrives in Tuba City. The Navajo Reservation is larger than many small countries, and it is difficult to remember that after driving for several hours you are still on the reservation.

At Tuba City, you can turn left onto Highway 264, which takes you on a spectacular drive across the high country of the Hopi mesas (including the Hopi Cultural Center complex on second mesa), and eventually drops you down in the direction of Winslow and Holbrook. If you proceed west from Tuba City, you will shortly intersect with the main north-south thoroughfare of Highway 89. A left-hand turn onto Highway 89 south will take

Traditional Navajo weaver, Navajo Reservation, Arizona.

you in the direction of the Grand Canyon and Flagstaff. A right-hand turn will head you in the direction the Lake Powell Recreation Area.

Back at Mexican Water, if you turn south on Highway 191 instead of proceeding west on Highway 160, Chinle, you arrive at the entrance to Canyon de Chelly National Monument. There are campgrounds, motels, restaurants, and other services available.

Heading south from Chinle, you eventually come to the Hubbell Trading Post Historic Site at Ganado, which has been maintained much as J.L. Hubbell left it. It is an active trading post, and there is also an interpretive center with ongoing weaving demonstrations by Navajo weavers. From Ganado you can proceed into Gallup and the Zuni area, or select a number of other destinations.

During the summer, it is possible to make the round trip from Cortez to Ganado in one full day, as long as one doesn't try to stop at every trading post along the way or spend more than a couple of hours in the Canyon de Chelly area. It is best, however, to slow down and really enjoy the Navajo lands. The Cortez Area Chamber of Commerce can help you to plan an exciting trip into the Navajo Reservation.

Heading south on Highway 666 also leads to Shiprock, and the great stone monolith that gives the location its name is clearly visible on the right.

In Shiprock, Highway 666 intersects with Highway 550 and State Route 504. Highway 555 goes east to Farmington and via Highway 64 from the middle of Farmington to the Salmon ruins. East of Farmington, Highway 550 comes to Aztec, and the highly interesting Aztec Ruins National Monument. From Aztec to Durango is slightly more than thirty miles, so this visit can be combined with Tour Route 8 as well.

Highway 44 leads south from Aztec toward to the Rio Grande Valley and intersects with I-25 at Bernalillo, New Mexico, between Sante Fe and Albuquerque. Highway 504 west from Shiprock connects up with Highway 160 at Teec Nos Pos, while continuing south on Highway 666 from Shiprock leads to Gallup and the east-west opportunities of I-40.

Chaco Canyon   The world-famous Chaco Culture National Historic Park, with its extensive Anasazi ruins and modern inter-

pretive center, is accessible by a variety of routes heading south from Cortez. Chaco Canyon can be visited in a
one-day trip. Drive south from Shiprock on Highway
666, and turn east just south of Tohatchi on the road to
Brimhall and Crownpoint; proceed from there to park
headquarters. From Aztec, go south on Highway 44 and
turn west at Blanco; this road is unpaved most of the
way and it is to be avoided during rainy or winter
weather. A somewhat more adventurous route takes you
straight south from Farmington on Highway 371. you
then turn east toward park headquarters just north of
Crownpoint. There are camping facilities, but no restaurants or motels in the park. Call park headquarters at
(505) 786-5384 for current road and other conditions.

Cortez is clearly the hub of the Anasazi area!

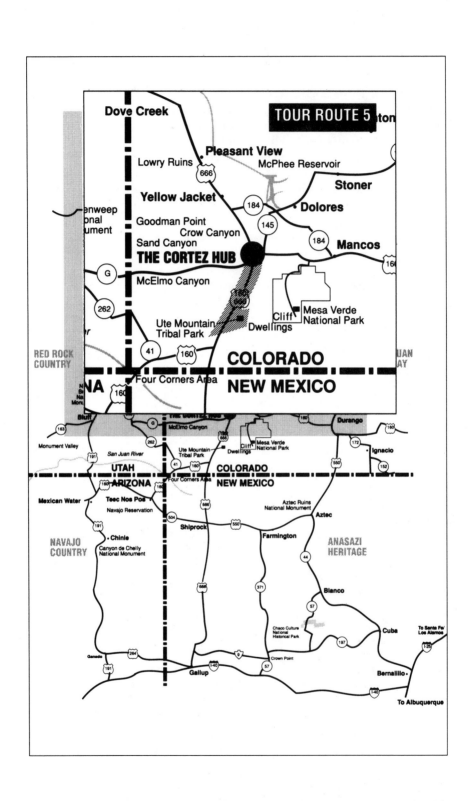

TOUR ROUTE 5
UTE MOUNTAIN TRIBAL PARK

▼ ▼ ▼ ▼ ▼ ▼ ▼ ▼

The Ute Mountain Tribal Park was established to preserve the ruins and provide access by the public. The Ute Indians lived in the canyons of Mesa Verde as late as the 1970s. Visitors have not had access to the many cliff dwellings on the reservation until just recently. The major ruins are now stabilized to prevent deterioration.

The Tribal Park was set aside by the tribe to preserve the prehistoric culture of the Anasazi who inhabited lands that are now part of the reservation. The modern Ute, however, are not direct descendants of the Anasazi. The park is located south of Mesa Verde National Park and encompasses approximately 125,000 acres centered along a twenty-five-mile stretch of the Mancos River. Hundreds of surface ruins and cliff dwellings are within the boundaries of the park, and a select number have been stabilized for visitation. Many historic Ute wall paintings and ancient petroglyphs can also be seen.

Mesa Verde National Park is so well-known that visitors often bypass the less well-known, but equally intriguing, Ute Mountain Tribal Park. The Tribal Park is twice the size of Mesa Verde and borders it on three sides. Both parks have hundreds of cliff dwellings and thousands of Anasazi ruins. To boost its economy, the Ute Mountain Ute Tribe is now trying to publicize the attractions of its tribal park.

The Tribal Park is operated as a primitive area in order to protect its cultural and environmental resources. Emphasis is on appreciating the natural setting, as well as visiting a number of the ruins that are in various stages of consolidation.

All tours are accompanied by a Ute Indian guide who interprets the park's archaeological and historic sites. Full-day tours begin at 9:00 AM at the Ute Mountain Pottery Plant, about fifteen miles south of Cortez on Highway 666/160. Reservations must be made by calling the Ute Mountain Tribal Park at (303) 565-3751, Extension 282, or (303) 565-4684.

Be sure to confirm your reservation before going to the Pottery Plant. You may ride a park vehicle to the main ruin sites and leave your vehicle at the Pottery Plant. It is a 110-mile round trip in the park and since all visits and tours are in remote areas, it is essential that you bring adequate gas, water, food, and comfortable clothes and shoes for hiking. From the Johnson Canyon Overlook you can see the archaeological sites of Eagles Nest, Morris 5, Lion House, and Tree House across the canyon. With a camera and a long lens, excellent photographs can be taken from this vantage point.

An optional activity is the descent of several long, sturdy ladders and many steps to reach the Main Ruins Trail. Here, in the ruins of Tree House, Lion House, Morris 5, and Eagles Nest, the prehistoric life of the Anasazi can be sensed and appreciated. The tour returns to the Pottery Plant between 4:00 and 5:00 PM.

A tour of Mesa Verde National Park will treat you to a grand history and an overview of the ancient Anasazi culture. A visit to the Ute Mountain Park will be an adventure into a unique area inhabited by the Anasazi of ancient times as well as modern-day Native Americans. Your guide will provide a personal perspective on traditional life, discussing the history of the Anasazi and the Ute Indians.

The present Ute Mountain Ute Reservation was formed in 1897 as the result of resistance by the Weminuche band of Utes to the U.S. government policy of forcing Native Americans to take individual allotments.

In 1895, the Weminuche left their Mouache and Capote cousins and established a camp on the western end of the old Southern Ute Reservation, in what is today known as Towaoc. Because of their relative isolation, the Ute Mountain Utes had little contact with the government or white settlers until comparatively recent times.

Ute handicraft has historically been in the form of beadwork, baskets, hide paintings, leatherwork, and some pottery. These items, produced for utilitarian purposes, are also the primary artistic expression of a nomadic people. The pottery produced is unique to this tribe. Although the designs may be similar to those of related Native American crafts, the originality of Ute Mountain pottery lies in its independent conception. Artists draw their inspiration from the contours and colors of their land. The temperament of these people, fashioned by the necessity of living directly from the earth, is reflected in each item.

Cliff dwellings, Ute Mountain Tribal Park.

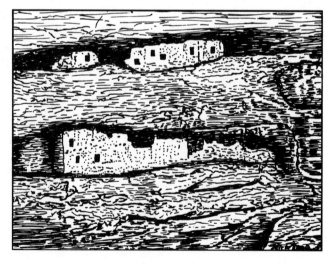

During the early part of summer, Ute Indians from around the area join the Ute Mountain Utes at the annual Bear Dance at Towaoc. The Bear Dance is celebrated as the time when the bear awakens from his winter hibernation. To the Utes, it is an occasion for celebrating the arrival of spring, and each year, people gather to renew acquaintances, meet new friends and to carry on courtships. Visitors are welcome and donations are appreciated for photos, which are permitted here. Check locally for exact dates.

Flight into the past. Helicopter rides at Ute Mountain Tribal Park.

More challenging and rigorous multiple-day backpacking trips and bicycle tours can also be arranged with advance planning.

A contract has been signed to offer helicopter tours of the Tribal Park. This tour offers an easy way to see the cliff houses, which are just as impressive as those of Mesa Verde. Four Corners Helicopter, Inc., offers three different tours of varying length. The heliport is reached through Mesa Verde National Park on Cliff Palace Road. Tours are from 9:00 AM to 5:00 PM and no reservations are necessary.

TOUR ROUTE 6
The Sleeping Ute, Mancos, and Mesa Verde

▼▼▼▼▼▼▼▼▼▼

Just east of Cortez, on the way to Mancos and Mesa Verde, is the best place to stop and see the imagery of Sleeping Ute Mountain, a prominent local landmark and focal point of a Native American legend. With some imagination, you can see the outline of a sleeping Indian, from his toes on the south, with peaks at his knees and with his arms folded over his chest. The form is best seen from a park just east of Cortez.

According to Ute legend, a great warrior god helped to fight against evil beings. There was a tremendous battle, and as they fought, their feet pushed the land into mountains and valleys. The great warrior god was hurt and lay down to rest, falling into a deep sleep. The blood from his wounds turned into water for all living creatures to drink. When fog or clouds settled over the god, it was a sign he was changing his blankets, dark green for summer, yellows and red for autumn, and white for winter. The Utes believe that when clouds gather on the highest peak, the warrior god is pleased with his people and letting rain clouds slip from his pockets. Archaeologists working in the area during the summer keep their raincoats at hand when there is a morning cloud over the tip of the Ute! The Native Americans believe the great warrior god will someday rise again to help them in the fight against their enemies.

Sleeping Ute Mountain

MANCOS

Between Cortez and the entrance to Mesa Verde National Park is the town of Mancos, which has a full range of tourist facilities. From the beautiful Mancos Valley (the one my daughter Kathy said she would buy if she had enough money!) there is a dramatic view of the 13,000-foot La Plata Mountains. Mancos was the first community settled in Montezuma County and has long been a center for cattle ranching. The Wetherill family, who first brought news of the cliff dwellings at Mesa Verde to the attention of the western world, had their ranch here. Jackson Lake and Bauer Lake, both excellent evening fishing spots, are only a few miles from town. Boyle Park has playground equipment and picnic tables.

FACILITIES   All telephone numbers use the 303 area code.

Motels

Budget Host Mesa Verde
191 West Railroad Avenue
533-7741

Enchanted Mesa Motel
862 West Grand Avenue
533-7729

Restaurant

Millwood Junction
Junction of Highway 160 and Main,
Mancos
533-7338

Bed and Breakfast

Tucker's Mountain Meadows
37951 Highway 184
533-7664

Located just west of Mesa Verde
National Park, with a view east to the
towering La Plata Range.

Ranch

Lake Mancos Ranch
2688 County Road North
533-7900
Easy-going vacation at its very best!

Campground

Trapper's Den Campground
37101 Highway 160, Mancos
533-7147

Mesa Verde National Park was established in 1906 as the first national park devoted to archaeological remains. In 1978 it was designated as the first World Heritage Site by the twenty-one-nation World Heritage Committee affiliated with the United Nations Education, Scientific, and Cultural Organization. Plan a full day or more to enjoy Mesa Verde, staying in the park itself or using Cortez as a base of operations.

MESA VERDE NATIONAL PARK

From the entrance, it takes at least forty-five minutes to the major ruins and museums. The trip is a very scenic one, with stupendous views of nearby mountains and four states. Elevation varies from 6,954 feet to 8,572 feet. Observe the posted speed limits and be alert for hikers, bicyclers, and deer. Local tales of flatlanders too timid to ascend the twisting park road, or who having made it up must be driven back down by a friendly ranger, should be judged on their merits *after* making the drive!

The first Native Americans entered the general Mesa Verde area about 2,000 years ago. By AD 500 they were building simple pit houses and making some pottery. By AD 850 the people were living in semisubterranean slab-walled villages. Building styles changed over the years until shortly after AD 1200, when almost all the mesa-top villages were abandoned. Some archaeologists believe that they may have done this for protection from other, hostile tribes. The cliff dwellings, however, have evidence of longer-term occupation that cast doubt on the defensive-strategy interpretation. One theory is that a drought in the late 1200s caused the inhabitants to abandon the cliff dwellings, and move south into the Rio Grande Valley in New Mexico.

To get the most out of your visit, start with either the Far View Visitor Center or the Chapin Mesa Museum. Rangers there will help you plan your visit. Some visitors like to view the ruins in chronological order, starting with the mesa-top ruins, then the museum, and finally the famous cliff dwellings.

Bicycles may be rented for touring the park. Hiking is restricted to a few designated areas, and hikers are required to register at the Chief Ranger's Office before taking either of the two trails off the Spruce Tree House Trail. The Petroglyph Point Trail is a 2.8-mile round trip and hikers can see petroglyphs, or rock art. The Spruce

Canyon Trail is 2.1 miles round trip and provides an opportunity to experience the canyon bottoms.

No permits are required for trails in the Morfield area, which provide views of the Montezuma and Mancos Valleys. The Prater Ridge Trail is 7.8 miles round trip. The Knife Edge Trail is 1.5 miles round trip, and the Point Lookout Trail is 2.3 miles round trip.

Morfield Campground provides a place to camp inside Mesa Verde, with 477 individual sites, and 17 group sites for up to 25 people each. No reservations are taken for individual sites, which are rarely full; reservations for

Cliff dwelling,
Mesa Verde
National Park

group sites are made through ARA Mesa Verde, P.O. Box 277, Mancos, CO 81328; telephone (303) 533-7731. An evening campfire program is offered by the National Park Service at 9:00 PM at the Morfield Campground amphitheater. During the summer, nondenominational religious services are also held. Check at the park for other special events.

Food, gasoline and lodging are available from mid-May to mid-October. Full interpretive services, with rangers at major sites and evening presentations, begin in mid-June and continue through Labor Day.

The entrance fee to Mesa Verde is $5 per carload, while tour groups pay $2 per person. A Golden Eagle Passport provides the holder and the immediate family with entrance to all national parks for one year. Free passes are available for handicapped and senior citizens 62 or older. Park rules prohibit entering a cliff dwelling without a park ranger. It is also forbidden to feed, capture, or tease wildlife or pick, cut, or damage any wildflower, shrub, or tree.

For more information, call (303) 529-4461 or 539-4475, or after hours 529-4463.

Mesa Verde can be divided into two general areas: the Far View/Wetherill Mesa area and the Chapin Mesa area.

FAR VIEW AND WETHERILL MESAS

The Wetherill Mesa ruins are open for self-guided or ranger-guided tours of cliff dwellings. The road, just west of the Far View Visitor Center, is open from 8:00 AM to 4:30 PM. The twelve-mile ride offers excellent views of the park and the Four Corners area. Vehicles in excess of 8,000 G.V.W. and/or twenty-five feet in length are prohibited.

Summer Activities

Wetherill Mesa offers a variety of sights, from cliff dwellings to mesa-top ruins. From the parking area, walk to the information kiosk and mini-train loading area. There, the ranger will help you plan your visit to the ruins.

Step House Ruin

This half-mile self-guided walk takes forty-five minutes to complete. Guidebooks are available on the trail to the ruin. A ranger is on duty in the dwelling to answer any questions. This ruin may be visited anytime between 9:15 AM and 5:15 PM.

Mini-Train

The mini-train departs from the kiosk area every half hour from 8:55 AM to 4:55 PM. There may be an hour wait for tours. You must ride the mini-train to visit the ranger-guided tour at Long House, the self-guided Badger House Community walk, the Kodak House Overlook, the Long House Overlook, and the Nordenskiold Ruin #16.

Long House   A ranger-guided tour of the park's second largest dwelling leaves every half hour from 9:00 AM to 5:00 PM at the trailhead. The total round-trip walking distance is a half mile and takes approximately one hour.

NOTE: Tours are limited to fifty people on a first come, first served basis. This tour is not recommended for those with physical limitations. The last tour to Long House leaves from the kiosk at 4:55 PM.

Badger House   This three-quarter-mile self-guided tour will take you
Community   to four mesa-top ruins; Modified Basketmaker Pithouse, Pueblo Village and Great Kiva, Badger House, and Two Raven House. Guidebooks are available at the beginning of the trail and a ranger will be roving the trail in order to answer any questions or provide assistance. This ruin may be visited anytime between 9:45 AM and 5:30 PM. Visitors taking the 5:00 tour (last tour) to Long House will not be able to visit Badger House or Step House.

Two Overlooks   Kodak House Viewpoint and Long House Overlook. Walking time to these view points is approximately fifteen minutes each.

CHAPIN   NOTE: The mini-train and most trails are accessible
MESA   by wheelchair. All hiking is restricted. Ask a ranger for hiking information. Smoking is restricted to the parking area. Pets are not allowed beyond the parking area. The ARA (concessioner) van departs from Far View Lodge at 8:30 AM. The Far View Lodge is the only motel inside the park.

Archaeological   Chapin Mesa offers self guided tours of large cliff
Museum   dwellings (including Cliff Palace) and mesa-top ruins and a ranger-guided tour of Balcony House.

The museum is open daily from 8:00 AM to 6:30 PM. Dioramas show the development stages of the Anasazi, and exhibits and artifacts explain the ancient way of life. Books can be purchased here, and bike rentals and other facilities are available. Spruce Tree House, close to the headquarters and museum, is the most easily accessible. Balcony House is enjoyed by many, but is reached via a thirty-two-foot ladder, and may not appeal to all.

Other sites may involve walking some distance. There is also a post office and first aid facility near the archaeological museum.

Later in the summer expect afternoon and evening rain (even deluges) and lightning storms across the mesa tops. Late September is cooler, a gorgeous and less-crowded time to visit Mesa Verde.

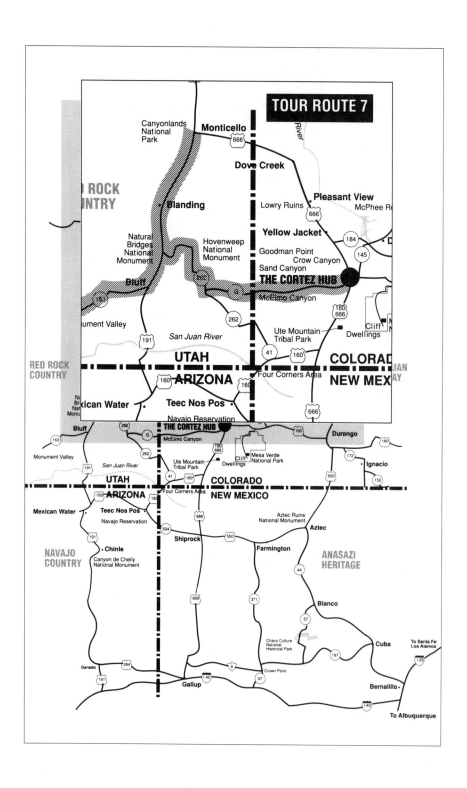

TOUR ROUTE 7
RED ROCKS COUNTRY

▼▼▼▼▼▼▼▼▼

West of Cortez, within a one-day round trip, are numerous opportunities to see some of the most spectacular red rocks country in the world. Again, each of these areas can provide many days, and even weeks, of enjoyment on their own. Cortez is an excellent place to jump off from or to use as headquarters while exploring the area. The following descriptions are designed to pique your interest. The Cortez Area Chamber of Commerce can provide more detailed information.

The red rocks country can be reached either by Tour Route 1 via Monticello, Utah, by Tour Route 3 to Hovenweep and Monticello, or by Tour Route 4, the Navajo-Hopi-Grand Canyon Gateway.

CANYONLANDS NATIONAL PARK

Canyonlands National Park consists of red rock canyons with intermittent stream beds. The park has spectacular views, natural arches and Anasazi Indian ruins and is ideal for hiking and backpacking. It is a two-hour drive from Cortez to the park entrance. The park can be enjoyed in one full day or several days can be spent exploring the area.

Newspaper Rock, Utah State Historical Monument

This monument contains petroglyphs spanning hundreds of years. The earliest were made by Navajos and Utes, and later additions were made by white settlers.

Confluence of the Green and Colorado Rivers

This drive offers a superb view of the confluence of the Green and Colorado Rivers, a thousand feet below. Both rivers wind through the red rock country to the Grand Canyon in Arizona.

Elephant Hill

This hill can only be reached by four-wheel-drive vehicle, on horseback, or by walking. Roads and trails on the other side of the hill offer spectacular views of the red rock country and access to the Colorado River.

Canyonland's Needles District

This area contains striking land forms of red and yellow sandstone rock eroded to needle-like forms by sand, wind, and rain.

Angel Arch   Angel Arch is a massive natural arch and is well
worth the hike or four-wheel-drive trip to see the arch
isolated and silhouetted against the sky.

Stone Arch,
Canyonlands
National Park

ARCHES   This National Park has the greatest concentration
NATIONAL   (over 500) of natural arches in the world. Some red-rock
PARK   sandstone formations can be seen from the road, others
can only be viewed from hiking trails. The Visitors Cen-
ter introduces the visitor to the park and its terrain and
paved roads lead to many of the spectacular arches. The
drive from Cortez is approximately two hours each way,
and views of numerous rock features, including Church
Rock, Wilson Arch, and the mountains called the Blues
and La Sals can be seen. There are twenty-one miles of
paved road that are open year-round and provide access to major points of interest, including the Windows
section, Balanced Rock, and Park Avenue.

Graded dirt roads lead to Wolfe Ranch and Klondike Bluffs, while numerous short trails lead to arches in the park, including a three-mile round trip to famed Delicate Arch. Ranger-guided hikes are conducted during the summer and there is a campground in the park; evening campfire programs are also conducted during the summer. Entrance and campground fees are collected at the Visitors Center, located at the entrance to the park, which is open year round.

Pinto Bean Paradise

During the growing season, the drive northwest from Cortez to the red rocks country takes the traveler through the heart of pinto bean country via Hovenweep or Monticello, Utah. The town of Dove Creek, on Highway 666 twenty-five miles northwest of Cortez, is famous as the "Pinto Bean Capital of the World," and is more thoroughly discussed in Tour Route 1. Views across pinto bean country to the east offer spectacular views of the San Juan Mountains, to the south to Mesa Verde National Park, to the southwest across Arizona and the Navajo Indian Reservation, and to the west across Utah. The Dolores River Overlook offers a impressive view of the river and its canyons.

Church Rock is located fifteen miles north of Monticello. The road from Monticello drops down into red sandstone country and Church Rock is the striking monument on the right side of the highway. This is just east of the entrance to Canyonlands National Park.

Wilson Arch is located thirteen miles past Church Rock, on the east side of the highway. A place to pull out and a rest area make the stop a safe and easy one. Wilson Arch is but a sample of the hundreds of arches to be seen at Arches National Park!

The Manti-La Sal National Forest and La Sal Mountain range have mountain peaks towering over 12,000 feet in elevation. A circle drive east from La Sal Junction, and up into the La Sal Mountains comes out a few miles south of the oasis of Moab, Utah. Aspen, blue spruce and pine trees, and deer and elk herds populate the mountains.

NATURAL BRIDGES

Natural Bridges National Monument is the only place in the United States where three immense natural bridge formations span impressive canyons. Trails lead the visitors to natural bridges which span up to 268 feet across, up to 220 feet high and 93 feet thick. The three main bridges were designated a national monument in 1908. This is a five-hour round trip drive from Cortez.

SAN JUAN RIVER   The drive along the San Juan River leads across the northern portion of the Navajo Indian Reservation, the largest reservation in the United States, with over 200,000 Navajo Indian residents. After traveling over part of the Aneth oil field, you come to historic Bluff, Utah. Here old Mormon settlers' homes and trading posts provide a glimpse into another century. Sand Island, along the shores of the San Juan River, has Anasazi Indian petroglyphs. Other points of interest on this one-day trip include the Valley of the Gods, with its red rock monuments and spires rising to the sky; the Goosenecks of the San Juan River, where millions of years of river meanders are frozen in stone over 1,000 feet below; and Mexican Hat, where the erosion of wind and rain have left this rock formation, balancing somewhat precariously, for all to see and to enjoy.

Sand Island   Sand Island has a large petroglyph panel on the sandstone cliffs along the San Juan River featuring Kokopelli, the humpbacked flute player, a notable figure in Pueblo Indian mythology. There are five Kokopellis on the panel on Sand Island.

Valley of the Gods   The seventeen-mile drive through the Valley of the Gods is a photographer's delight, with monoliths resembling a miniature Monument Valley. During the summer, a late afternoon storm can add excitement to the landscape, while a winter mantle of white can also emphasize the shadows and subtleties of the geological formations. The formations jut hundreds of feet into the air, and the figures of the valley are imaginary animals, gods, or whatever else the mind's eye can see.

Goosenecks State Reserve   This area contains one of the most impressive examples of entrenched river meanders in the North American continent. The 1,500-foot deep meanders were cut by the San Juan River, whose headwaters are in the San Juan Mountains of southwestern Colorado. From there it cuts across the northwest corner of New Mexico, marking the northern boundary of the Navajo Reservation in southern Utah, and finally becomes part of Lake Powell forty miles downstream.

Mexican Hat

The Mexican Hat area of the San Juan River offers many colorful attractions, including Mexican Hat Rock and Navajo Rug. The latter is the name for the wavy patterns of the rock strata on the cliff behind the Mexican Hat Rock, which are similar to the geometric designs of many Navajo textiles.

Visitor facilities in Blanding, Bluff, and Monticello have already been listed in the sections on Tours 1 and 3.

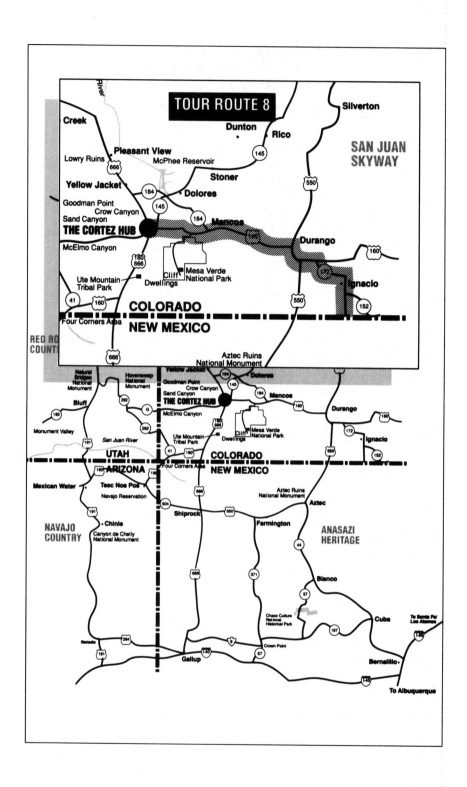

TOUR ROUTE 8
DURANGO GATEWAY

▼▼▼▼▼▼▼▼

Durango has a wide variety of facilities, from carefully maintained Victorian neighborhoods to a narrow gauge railroad. Durango is also the home of Fort Lewis College, with its well-known Center for Southwest Studies. A host of cultural events occur at the college throughout the year. Old-fashioned carriage rides are available for a casual visit to the elegantly restored and maintained National Historic District Victorian section of town.

Hikers will enjoy the recently completed Colorado Trail, which starts (or ends) in Durango and winds its way for 482 miles through the mountains to Denver. Summer water sports and winter skiing opportunities abound in the mountains near Durango. The world-famous Purgatory Ski Area also has a summer theater program and other year-round activities, including a giant alpine slide.

Eighteen miles northeast of Durango is lovely Vallecito Lake. Deer, elk, and other wildlife delight the eye and entice the photographer. Cabins, lodges, and camping are all available, and activities include horseback riding, fishing, boating, and hiking. Just sitting and contemplating the high mountains and gorgeous sunsets is also permissible! Approaching Durango from the east on Highway 160, Vallecito is reached by turning north at Bayfield and following the sign; if you are coming from the west, take the Highway 160 bypass around Durango and turn north at Bayfield. If you are already in Durango, take Florida Avenue northeast out of town.

FACILITIES   All telephone numbers use the 303 area code.

For detailed information on Durango, call the Durango Area Chamber Resort Association, toll free:
800-358-8855 Colorado
800-525-8855 Nationwide

Motels and Hotels

Thirty-nine motels and hotels, including the historic General Palmer and Strater hotels, and three Bed and Breakfast facilities offer a wide range of facilities and prices.

Restaurants

The restaurants of Durango present a variety of cuisines and prices.

Campgrounds and RV Parks

The Durango area boasts eight parks and campgrounds.

Museums and Galleries

Animas School Museum,
La Plata County Historical Society.
31st and West 2nd Avenue
(303) 259-2042

The downtown district has a wide range of shops and galleries. The Toh Atin Gallery, which has a branch gallery in the same building as the Mesa Verde Pottery plant on the eastern edge of Cortez, has its main gallery in Durango, located at 145 West 9th. Call toll free: 800-322-5799 in Colorado and 800-525-0384 nationwide.

Other Attractions and Services

Durango and Silverton Narrow Gauge Railroad
479 Main Street
(303) 247-2733

The D&SNG Railroad Company has pledged ". . . to preserve the history and authenticity of the Railroad, (and) to operate in the truest of railroad tradition. . ." The trains operate seasonally from early May to mid-October.

Narrow gauge railroad, Durango

IGNACIO

Ignacio is located about twenty-five miles southeast of Durango on Highway 172. The facilities in Ignacio are all part of one tribal complex and are concentrated in one location.

Motel and Restaurant

Sky Ute Lodge and Restaurant
(303) 563-4531 (Use this telephone number for other listed attractions as well.)

Museum

Southern Ute Cultural Center and Museum

Other Attractions

Sky Ute Gallery
Southern Ute buffalo herd
Interpretive program by tribal elders
Traditional Native American dances

Other Services

Groceries, camping, and automotive supplies are also available.

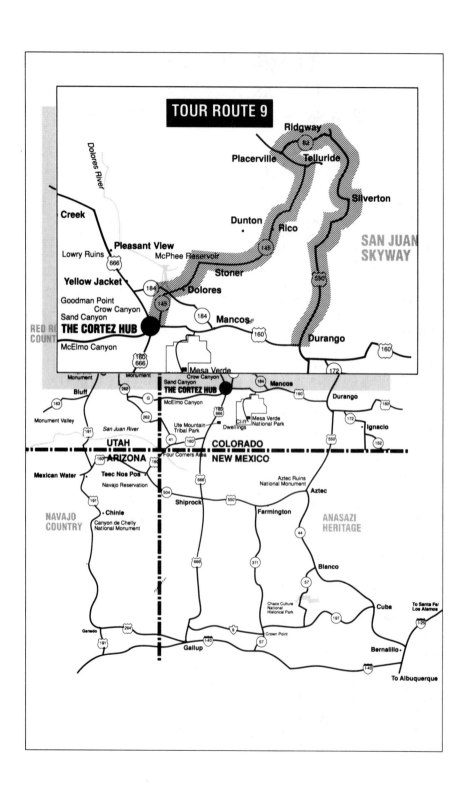

TOUR ROUTE 9

SAN JUAN SKYWAY

Ridgway

Placerville   Telluride

Silverton

Dunton   Rico   145

Creek

Pleasant View

Lowry Ruins   666   McPhee Reservoir

Yellow Jacket   184   Stoner   550

Goodman Point
Crow Canyon   145   Dolores
Sand Canyon   184   Mancos

THE CORTEZ HUB   160   Durango

RED R_
COUNT_   McElmo Canyon   160
                           160
                           666

160
Mesa Verde   172

Monument   Monument   Crow Canyon   Sand Canyon   184   Mancos
                                                                                160   Durango   160

Bluff   262   G   THE CORTEZ HUB

                       McElmo Canyon   180   172   Ignacio
                                         666
163   Monument Valley   Mesa Verde   550   152
                                        National Park

191   San Juan River   Ute Mountain   Cliff
                         Tribal Park   Dwellings
                         41   160
UTAH   COLORADO
ARIZONA   164   Four Corners Area   NEW MEXICO

Mexican Water   Teec Nos Pos   504   666   Aztec Ruins   Aztec
                 Navajo Reservation   550   National Monument

191   Chinle   Shiprock   Farmington   ANASAZI
NAVAJO   Canyon de Chelly   HERITAGE
COUNTRY   National Monument   44

                         666   371   Blanco

                                         57

                    Chaco Culture   197   Cuba   To Santa Fe/
                    National   Los Alamos
264   Ganado   Historical Park   I-25
                         9   Crown Point
191   40   57   Bernalillo
       Gallup   I-40
                         To Albuquerque

TOUR ROUTE 9
THE SAN JUAN SKYWAY

One of the advantages of the Greater Cortez Area is the proximity of the semiarid plateaus and the cool forested mountains. Both can be explored and enjoyed during even a brief visit. From Cortez, Dolores is the gateway to the mountains.

The San Juan Skyway is Colorado's first National Forest Scenic Byway; some consider the Skyway one of the most spectacular drives in America. This approximately 240-mile loop can be made in one day, or stretched over several days. During summer the mountain scenery and permanent snowpacks are beautiful, but try fall (September 15 through October 15) for spectacular colors. The loop may be initiated from Cortez, from Durango, or many other points of access along the route. Roads are paved all the way, and there are plenty of opportunities to pull off, breathe the fresh mountain air, listen to rushing brooks, and photograph the wildflowers, animals, mountain ranches, and Victorian buildings and houses. Points of interest are spread along the route and include fishing areas; prehistoric ruins; old mining camps; and camping, hiking, skiing, and recreational areas. Forest Service offices sell audiotapes about the loop and can provide additional information on points of interest and current conditions.

DOLORES

Coming from Cortez, the first community to be encountered is Dolores, along the river of the same name and adjacent to the McPhee Reservoir. Visitor facilities in Dolores are listed in the section on Tour Route 2. We will concentrate here on the spectacular scenery that greets you as you head through town and up the Dolores River valley towards Stoner, Rico, and Telluride.

The Dolores River

The white-water adventures and striking scenery of the Dolores River are becoming more widely known each year. Thirty commercial rafting companies operate trips on the river and together with private use they totaled almost 10,000 user-days last year.

Humpback Chub River Tours offers three-day trips between Bradfield Bridge and Slick Rock or between Slick Rock and Bedrock. A seven-day trip is offered from Bradfield Bridge to Bedrock. One-day trips are also available. The sixteen-foot rafts can carry six people. For more information, call (303) 882-7940.

Current information on river flow is available form the Bureau of Land Management, (303) 882-7600. Private groups need no permits, but commercial operators are required to obtain a BLM permit.

Rafters are requested to use the Bradfield Bridge put-in if floating the river downstream from the McPhee Reservoir and to sign in at the river register box there. River register boxes are also available for put-in or take-out at the Dove Creek Pump Station, at Slick Rock, at Gypsum Valley, and at Bedrock. These procedures are both to monitor river use and for rafters' safety.

Most rafters put in at the Bradfield Bridge, six miles below the McPhee Dam. From there a one-day trip takes you to the Dove Creek pump station and a seven-day trip takes you to Bedrock. The trip below the Bradfield Bridge is exciting and there is great variety in both water and landscape. You float along slowly, enjoying the scenery for awhile; then in other stretches, the ride is wilder. Signs of modern civilization soon disappear, but there are Anasazi ruins and ancient rock art along the way. Observant rafters may even spot bighorn sheep and river otters, recently reintroduced by the Colorado Division of Wildlife.

All river users are asked to carry porta-potties and to use fire pans for overnight trips. For more information on river floating and rafting, contact the BLM at 701 Camino del Rio, Durango, CO 81301, or call (303) 247-4082.

A scenic drive along the Dolores River valley at any time of the year reveals stupendous scenery. A Forest Service brochure notes that the Dolores River Canyon, is 2,000 to 2,600 feet deep and carries the same general shape and coloration as the Grand Canyon.

From Dolores, head northeast on Highway 145; the highway follows the Dolores River the entire way. About twelve miles north of Dolores, just before the town of Stoner, turn off on Forest Service Road 535, known locally as the Dunton Road. Dunton Road follows the scenic West Fork of the Dolores River.

Hard winters and primitive conditions require road repairs from time to time, so check local information before embarking on these and similar routes.

West Fork   The West Fork has splendid mountain valley scenery and fishing. In the fall, the golden aspen contrast with the dark green evergreen, to the delight of camera enthusiasts. Hunters can find plenty of big game here, too. Furthermore, the only active geyser in Colorado can be reached on Forest Service trail 548, which takes off south of Dunton.

If roads are dry, proceed north of the Burro Bridge campground and cross the meadows, which are carpeted with colorful wildflowers, especially in June. Passenger cars can traverse this dirt and gravel road in dry weather, with caution, but trailers and motorhomes are discouraged. You'll reconnect with Highway 134 north of Rico. From there you can drive north for five miles on Highway 145 to Lizard Head Pass at an elevation of 10,222 feet. The pass got its name from a distinctive rock formation named by earlier travelers.

Rico, a Spanish word meaning "rich," was named for the fabulous fortunes of silver and gold found in the nearby mines during the early 1880s. At that time this roaring little boomtown had a population of 5,000 and reportedly never slept. Now the mines are closed, but a more permanent kind of treasure comes from the grandeur of seven mountain peaks, the lush meadows, and rushing mountain streams. Gasoline, postal, antique stores, groceries, and cafe services are available in Rico. A new era of tourist and vacation development is underway, and prosperity seems poised to return to Rico. The Galloping Goose Bar and Restaurant on the northern edge of Rico has a wide variety of beer and liquor and a menu for varied tastes. The Enterprise Bar and Grill on Main Street is open only during the summer season.

RICO

Between Rico and Telluride you pass Trout Lake, which has an absolutely fantastic setting, nestled at the base of high mountains that, even toward the end of June, are still largely snow-covered.

Just below Trout Lake is the Ames Power Plant, which almost a century ago became the first utility in the country to supply industrial users with alternating electric current. In 1988, the plant was honored as a Historical Electrical Engineering Milestone by the Pikes Peak Section of the Institute of Electrical and Electronic Engineers.

TELLURIDE   A day trip from Cortez to Telluride is yet another encounter with spectacular scenery. Highway 145 takes
the traveler from Cortez and Rico through some of the
most spectacular scenery the silvery San Juan Mountains
have to offer. The town of Telluride is a National Historic District; during the winter, it is a major ski resort
with the longest ski lift in the world (two and a half
miles). The town is nestled in a mountain valley at 9,000
feet elevation, surrounded by 14,000-foot high mountain
peaks. Whether you are a winter or summer visitor, the
scenery is unsurpassed. Telluride is also the festival cap-

Skier at Telluride.

ital of Colorado. The International Film Festival, Blue-
grass, and Jazz Festivals, hang-gliding competitions, and
ski competitions make Telluride an exciting place for
everyone year round.

Telluride is accessible by road or by air. Mesa Airlines has one daily flight to Telluride from Albuquerque,
and during the winter ski season also offers one flight
daily from Phoenix. Call the Mesa reservation number
(800-637-2247) for schedule details.

The high country beauty, ski, and festival activities
of Telluride combined with the archaeological enchant-
ments of the Cortez area, are the ingredients for the per-
fect vacation anytime of the year.

Telluride has retained its Victorian atmosphere, and the unique shops, restaurants, and condominiums reflect this charm. A gondola ride from the base of Coonskin Run (right in town) takes you up to the world-class Mountain Village Resort. Here is some of the best skiing in the Rocky Mountains. Golfers will enjoy the new eighteen-hole golf course. The combination of the old and the new makes Telluride truly distinctive.

San Miguel County Museum

The county's mining and ranching days are celebrated in this historical collection of turn-of-the-century artifacts. The museum is located at the top of Fir Street. The telephone number is (303) 728-3344.

After Telluride, the route drops to Placerville, then to Ridgway on Highway 550 to head south to Ouray, Silverton, the Purgatory Ski Area, Durango, Mancos, and back to Cortez. All of the old mining communities have retained their Victorian charm. Silverton is the terminus of the Durango and Silverton Narrow Gauge Railroad that originates in Durango (Tour Route 8). There are extensive visitor facilities in these communities, and the scenery is spectacular. During the late fall and winter, be sure to check road conditions before heading into the mountains; conditions can change rapidly as storms develop.

Frequently referred to as the Million Dollar Highway, the route from Ridgway to Durango crosses a number of passes with elevations in excess of 10,000 feet. You may need to stop to enjoy the scenery, or share the driving with someone and take turns looking!

We want you to keep returning to the Cortez hub and the Four Corners area until you have sampled all of the nine tours in this guide, or, even better, invented many more of your own.

SUGGESTED READINGS

General Interest

Abbott, Carl, Stephen J. Leonard, and David McComb
1982   *Colorado: A History of the Centennial State.* Boulder, CO: Colorado Associated University Press.

Boddie, Caryn and Peter
1984   *The Hiker's Guide to Colorado.* Billings and Helena, MT: Falcon Press.

Brown, Robert L.
1987   *Colorado Ghost Towns: Past and Present.* Caldwell, ID: The Caxton Printers.

Chronic, Halka
1980   *Roadside Geology of Colorado.* Missoula, MT: Mountain Press.

Caughey, Bruce and Dean Winstanley
1989   *The Colorado Guide: Landscapes, Cityscapes, Escapes.* Golden, CO: Fulcrum.

Gregory, Lee
1990   *Colorado Scenic Guide: Southern Region.* Revised edition. Boulder, CO: Johnson Books.

McTighe, Jack
1989   *Roadside History of Colorado.* Boulder, CO: Johnson Books.

General Overview of Southwestern and Colorado Prehistory

Ambler, Richard
1977   *The Anasazi.* Photographs by Marc Gaede. Flagstaff: Museum of Northern Arizona. This is a well rounded introduction to the Anasazi, written in a nontechnical style.

Cassells, Steve E.
1983   *The Archaeology of Colorado.* Boulder, CO: Johnson Books. This is the most up-to-date overview on the prehistory of Colorado. It also contains interesting biographical sketches of a number of prominent Colorado archaeologists.

Cordell, Linda
1984   *The Prehistory of the Southwest.* San Diego: Academic Press. This is the most recent survey on prehistory and archaeology of the southwest, written with a textbook approach.

Muench, David and Donald G. Pike
1974   *Anasazi: Ancient People of the Rock.* New York: Crown. An enjoyable description of the Anasazi with very nice photography. Emphasizes architecture and social organization, rather than portable artifacts.

Ortiz, Alfonso (editor)
1979   *Handbook of North American Indians, Vol. 9 .* Washington, D.C.: Smithsonian. Several of the chapters in this volume are devoted to the prehistory of the Southwest, and provide short, concise overviews of the region.

Lange, Frederick W. and Diana Leonard (editors)
1985   *Among Ancient Ruins: The Legacy of Earl Morris.* Boulder, CO: Johnson Books. This book depicts the life of Earl H. Morris, an early southwestern archaeologist, and his work through original photographs.

Lange, Frederick, Nancy Mahaney, Joe Ben Wheat,
Mark L. Chenault, John Cater
1988   *Yellow Jacket: A Four Corners Anasazi Ceremonial Center.* Boulder, CO: Johnson Books (rev. ed.).

Malville, J. McKim
1989   *Prehistoric Astronomy of the Southwest.* Boulder, CO: Johnson Books.

Wheat, Joe Ben
1954   MT-1, A Basketmaker III Site Near Yellow Jacket Colorado (Progress Report). *Southwestern Lore* 21:18-26.

1980   Yellow Jacket Canyon Archaeology. In *Insights into the Ancient Ones,* edited by J. and East Berger, 60-66. Cortez, CO: Mesa Verde Press.

1981   Anasazi Who? In *Anasazi Symposium,* edited by J. Smith, 11-15. Mesa Verde National Park, CO: Mesa Verde Museum Association, Inc.

Four Corners Archaeology

INDEX

Silverton, Colorado 85
Skiing, *see* Winter Sports
Sleeping Ute Legend 63
Smith, Jack 20
Smithsonian Institution 50
Southern Ute Tribe 78-79
Southern Ute Cultural Center and Museum 79
Spanish Explorers 18, 44
Stoner, Colorado 81
Swedish National Museum 18

Teec Nos Pos, New Mexico 53, 56
Telluride, Colorado 16-17, 43, 79, 81, 83-85
Tohatchi, New Mexico 57
Totten Lake, *see* McPhee Reservoir and
    Recreation Area
Tours, *see* Anasazi Tours
Towaoc, Colorado 60
Travel Tips 14
Trout Lake 83
Tuba City, Arizona 55

University of Colorado 3, 20-21
    see also Cortez CU Center
    see also Yellow Jacket Archaeological Site
Ute Indians 1-2, 47, 63, 71
    Weminuche Band 60

Ute Mountain Ute Tribe 59-60
    Bingo 9
    Pottery Factory 53, 59-60
    Tribal Park 59-61
Ute Mountain 16

Vallecito Lake, *see* Durango, Colorado
Valley of the Gods 74

Water Sports
    see Bauer Lake
    see Dolores, Colorado
    see Durango, Colorado (Vallecito Lake)
    see Jackson Lake
    see Lake Powell Recreation Area
    see McPhee Reservoir and Recreation Area
    see Trout Lake
Wetherill Family 18, 20, 64
Wheat, Joe Ben 20
Winslow, Arizona 55
Winter Sports 15-17, 37, 77, 84-85

Yellow Jacket
    Archaeological Site iii, 3-4, 20-21, 25-27,
        32, 34-35
    Area 33-34, 36

Zuni Pueblo, New Mexico 56